Growing Up Sad

GROWING UP SAD

Childhood Depression and Its Treatment

LEON CYTRYN, M.D.

DONALD H. MCKNEW, JR., M.D.

W. W. NORTON & COMPANY

New York • London

Dr. Cytryn is contributing his royalties on this book to the Holocaust Museum in Washington, D.C.

First published as a Norton paperback 1998

The text of this book is composed in Veljovic Book with the display set in Veljovic Bold Italic and Globe True Condensed.
Composition and manufacturing by the Haddon Craftsmen
Book design by Charlotte Staub

Library of Congress Cataloging-in-Publication Data

Cytryn, Leon.
    Growing up sad: childhood depression and its treatment / Leon Cytryn, Donald H. McKnew.
        p.   cm.
    Based on the authors' : Why isn't Johnny crying?   1983.
    Includes bibliographical references and index.
    ISBN 0-393-03827-0
    1. Depression in children.   I. McKnew, Donald H.   II. McKnew, Donald H.   Why isn't Johnny crying?   III. Title.
RJ506.D4C97 1996
618.92'8527—dc20   95-41233   CIP

ISBN 0-393-31788-9 pbk.

        W. W. Norton & Company, Inc.
    500 Fifth Avenue, New York, N.Y. 10110
            www.wwnorton.com

        W. W. Norton & Company Ltd.
Castle House, 75/76 Wells Street, London W1T 3QT

    4 5 6 7 8 9 0

*In loving memory of
all my family members
who perished during
the Holocaust
      Leon Cytryn*

*To all my family
      Donald McKnew*

Foreword

The first version of this book—*Why Isn't Johnny Crying?*—appeared in 1983 as a comprehensive consolidation of what was known and conceptualized to that time about depression beginning in childhood. It represented a biopsychosocial synthesis, combining the authors' own extensive research and clinical experience with many other earlier findings and theoretical points of view.

As recently as 25 years ago it was possible to actively debate the validity—indeed, the very existence—of depression as a definable diagnostic disorder in children, comparable to depression in adults. Cytryn and McKnew first proposed a diagnostic classification of childhood depression in 1972. A chapter on the psychopharmacology of childhood affective disorders appeared in 1977 in a book I edited on the *Psychopharmacology of Childhood and Adolescent Disorders,* but it was not until the publication of *DSM-III* in 1980 that childhood-onset depression was described and established as an official diagnostic entity with signs and symptoms essentially the same as or similar to those in adults.

Of course, depression qua sadness in children—even in infants—had long been recognized and identified. René Spitz described anaclitic depression and "hospitalism" in infants as a result of inadequate emotional caretaking, as well as marked sadness in response to separation after an attachment to the mother had developed. John Bowlby described the sequence of protest, despair, and detachment following separation occasioned by hospitalization, and James Robertson made a dramatic film of a two-year-old in the hospital. In so doing they revolutionized the "no visitors" (including parents) policy then almost universal in pediatric wards and in children's hospitals. Despite these and other clinically astute observations of the phenomenology of childhood depression, recognition of the disorder of depression per se was held back by the prevailing psychoanalytic theory of mental structure and beliefs about the psychodynamics of depression, which taken together proposed that depression as it was understood in adults could not occur in children. This shows how a powerful and coherent theory, which had provided illumination and insight, also led to resistance and blind spots.

Eventually, psychoanalytic theory was overtaken by increasingly important biological explanations and descriptive diagnostic criteria, which came together during the 1970s. Since then research, clinical experience, and literature on childhood-onset depression have grown enormously, explicating, for example, the phenomenology, epidemiology, role of genetic predisposition, influences of family structure and childhood temperament, importance of early separation or loss, and prognosis and life course of the disorder. The insights into neurochemistry gained from psychopharmacology have opened doorways to more specific and targeted treatments, both by medication alone and in combination with psychosocial interventions.

Leon Cytryn and Don McKnew have not only made major contributions to the advances and developments in our understanding of childhood depression but also applied themselves to the task of integrating our knowledge into meaningful biopsychosocial constructs. This effort on their part is reflected in the content and sequencing of this book's chapters, from "Dawn of Discovery" at the beginning to "Prevention" and "Cutting Edge" at the end. A worthy sequel to and expansion of the earlier edition, *Growing Up Sad* will be of value to all professionals who care about and try to help children deal with depression and realize their maximum developmental potential.

Jerry M. Wiener, M.D.
Leon Yochelson Professor and Chairman,
Department of Psychiatry & Behavioral
Sciences, and Professor of Pediatrics,
The George Washington University
School of Medicine

Contents

Preface

Several converging factors encouraged us to update our 1983 work on childhood depression, *Why Isn't Johnny Crying?*, on which this book is based. In the last decade, clinicians and researchers have made significant advances in the diagnosis, treatment, and prevention of mood disorders in all age groups, ranging from the very young to the increasing ranks of the aging population.

In the treatment area, the introduction of new classes of antidepressant drugs, coupled with the recognition of the frequent need to combine several of such drugs, based on enhanced understanding of mood disorders, has offered new hope to those afflicted with depressive illness. Yet this success has been clouded by the failure of many rigorous studies to demonstrate the effectiveness of antidepressants in the treatment of children and adolescents. These findings, which fly in the face of the enthusiastic endorsements by clinicians, pose challenges that will keep sophisticated researchers busy in the years ahead.

The profession is also beginning to understand mood disorders as part of the developmental processes of the person. Instead of viewing mood disorders in children in isolation from mood disorders in adults, we now attempt to understand the different clinical manifestations of depressive disorders in different age groups. This approach throws new light on the question of continuity of mood disorders across the life span.

In addition, new epidemiological findings have clarified the coexistence of depression with other mental disorders, which so challenged our diagnostic process in the past. We can now see that comorbidity of mood disorders with other psychiatric entities is highly prevalent in both adults and children. Although the large-scale, multicenter epidemiological studies of the prevalence of depression in the general population have excluded children and adolescents, efforts are underway to rectify this, so that soon we will be able to assess more accurately the prevalence of depression in the younger members of our society.

Another problem that already has provoked and will continue to stimulate vigorous discussion and research is the apparent increase in the incidence of depressive disorders in children. Is this increase only apparent, due to the refinement of our diagnostic instruments and increased acceptance of the existence of clinical depression in children? Or are we witnessing a real increase in the incidence of this malady, due to intensification of environmental stresses in our society?

The parallel increase of reported suicide attempts in young children challenges the long-held view within the field of psychiatry that, while suicidal ideation in prepubertal children is common, suicide attempts in this age group are very rare. The ongoing investigation of these phenomena will no doubt elucidate the role of environmental, social factors in the genesis of depressive disorders. Of particular interest are research efforts attempting to clarify how environmental pressures lead to psychological reactions and how those eventually translate into biochemical changes, which form the endpath and the core of depressive illness.

Other important research findings indicate that: (1) childhood depression may be more serious than we believed in the past; (2) it is often followed by multiple recurrences; and (3) though mostly unipolar, it is a frequent forerunner of a bipolar disorder (manic-depression) in adolescence or young adulthood.

All this being the case, vigorous treatment is urgently recommended once depression in a child is diagnosed. We must avoid our tendency to consider depressive manifestations as possible "stages" in a child's development. A fascinating hypothesis, the "kindling" phenomenon in depressive illness, postulates that each recurrence of a depressive episode has a more serious clinical course than its predecessor. It is to be hoped that early and vigorous treatment, followed by appropriate aftercare, will prevent such recurrences or at least reduce their clinical severity.

Additionally, one must mention the recent increased emphasis on *prevention* of depression, as well as other mental disorders. Striking successes in preventing cardiovascular disorders, accidents, and lung cancer, to mention just a few, serve as models for the field of mental health. Mood disorders reduce the quality of life at any age, severely circumscribe the functioning of those afflicted, and cause tremendous hardships to the patients and their families, as well as enormous financial burdens to society at large.* Let us hope that the next decade will witness the expansion of fledgling modest attempts at prevention of depressive disorders, leading to formal and vigorous public mental health protective measures, akin to inoculations to prevent infectious diseases.

Finally, let us remember that depression is a part of human condition, a result of many varied causes. It would be unrealistic to expect a total eradication of depressive illness. However, we may realistically aim at significant reduction of its painful impact on the lives of millions of children and their families.

Acknowledgments

During the years that we have studied the problems discussed in this book, we have been encouraged, helped, and guided by a number of farsighted colleagues. We would like to single out four of them for mention: Dr. Reginald Lourie, Dr. Joseph Noshpitz, Dr. Jerry Wiener, and Dr. William E. Bunney, Jr. We would

---

* A Massachusetts Institute of Technology study revealed that almost $44 billion is lost every year in the U.S. economy because depression goes undiagnosed and untreated and causes lost job productivity.

like to thank our late friend and coauthor, Herbert Yahraes, for his contribution to the writing and preparation of *Why Isn't Johnny Crying?* We would like to thank Dr. Eileen Cytryn and Marsha Shaw for their help in editing and preparing the manuscript. We also want to acknowledge the generous support of our publisher, W. W. Norton & Company, especially its former editor Donald Fusting and our present editor Susan Barrows Munro, without whose perseverance and attentiveness this task could not have been completed.

Leon Cytryn, M.D.
Donald H. McKnew, Jr., M.D.

Growing Up Sad

ONE

Childhood Depression — The Dawn of Discovery

It's a coming-and-going thing. I don't feel depressed all the time. Usually it takes something, no matter how minor, to really set it off, and I start feeling bad about something and I can't do anything, and so today everything's been going pretty well, so I don't feel bad at all. But on another day, you know, I might just not want to get up in the morning or do anything at all . . . just like everything's worthless, like it's just not worth it to even be. That's about the best I can do. It's—it seems like it's a silly thing to even go through life and exist. And from one day to the next you're always wondering if you're going to make it to the next day if it's—if you can stand it, if it's worth trying to get to tomorrow. . . . It's just—just, I feel like—I feel mostly like I'm worthless, like there's something wrong with me. It's really not a pleasant feeling to know that you're a total failure, a complete nothing, and I get the feeling that I didn't do nothing right or worthwhile or anything.

Depression in adults is a sad, lonely, and at times tragic experience. In children it can be even more devastating, as illustrated by these words of a teenage boy.

Nowadays we can speak of childhood depression, but not long ago, no one, in or out of the psychiatric profession, did so.

For historic reasons, in part related to Sigmund Freud's legacy, the psychiatric profession simply had no official classification for children whose behaviors and moods mimicked "adult" depression—that is, not until a couple of observers separately noticed a similar phenomenon.

Quite some time ago, in the late 1950s, as a young pediatrician, one of the authors, Leon Cytryn, was struck by the frequency of sadness and withdrawal in preadolescent and early adolescent boys who were admitted to a pediatric hospital for a surgical repair of undescended testicles (cryptorchism). This observation led to a research project to explore the emotional adjustment of children with this specific condition. The results of the study indicated that of the boys with undescended testicles, especially those in whom the surgical repair was delayed beyond the age of eight years, almost half were seriously emotionally disturbed. Of those, most had symptoms closely associated with adult depression, such as sad mood, poor self-esteem, social withdrawal, poor school performance, and a feeling of hopelessness.[1]

Intrigued by these findings, Cytryn collaborated in studies exploring the emotional adjustment of children with four types of chronic illness: cystic fibrosis, congenital heart disease, sickle-cell anemia, and congenital amputation. In each of these illnesses, except for congenital amputation, the findings were similar to those in the previous study of boys with undescended testicles. Close to half of the children showed symptoms of emotional disturbance characterized by depressive symptoms (sadness, withdrawal, impairment in functioning, social isolation, helplessness, and hopelessness) and/or symptoms of anxiety (separation anxiety, fear of strangers, phobic avoidance, tension, irritability, and sleep disturbances).[2,3]

Several years later, in the early 1960s, Cytryn, by now a pediatric psychiatrist, returned to a large pediatric university hospital. His duties there included making teaching rounds biweekly on the pediatric and surgical wards, accompanied by medical students, interns, and residents. The children seen by Cytryn either suffered from a medical illness or had come there for surgery. None had been previously diagnosed as having an emotional disorder.

Yet many of these physically ill children appeared to be markedly depressed, according to all the criteria used at that time to diagnose adult depression. Puzzled, Cytryn wondered if they did not, in fact, suffer from the same condition that afflicted depressed adults or, at the least, from a related condition. Furthermore, he wondered whether such a depressive condition might exist in children who do not have a concomitant physical illness or handicap and who have never been hospitalized. At the time, it was thought that children did not suffer from depression.

At the time, Donald McKnew was also working with hospitalized children, in a large hospital in another city. Here the children were not physically ill or injured; rather, they were in a mental hospital, having been admitted for a variety of reasons. Two diagnoses predominated. One was schizophrenia, the name given to a group of disorders marked by psychotic thinking. The other principal diagnosis was conduct disorder, wherein patients exhibit a variety of antisocial behaviors.

Like Cytryn, McKnew was impressed by his observation that a number of the children he encountered were extremely sad, withdrawn, and lethargic most of the time and expressed feelings of low self-esteem, hopelessness, and despair. He, too, wondered whether these children might not suffer from depression, either as their main illness or secondary to their presenting illness or simply because they were in a hospital.

Both McKnew and Cytryn were aware that a diagnosis of childhood depression was not acceptable to the medical profession in those days; medical teaching still insisted that children did not become depressed in a clinical sense. Even so, McKnew wanted to test his observations further. It was known at the time that depressed adults had increased blood cortisol levels. That being the case, could he not test the blood of these seemingly depressed children to see if they, too, had similar abnormal blood cortisol levels? He attempted to elicit the cooperation of the endocrinology department in order to study these biochemical abnormalities known to exist in depressed adults. Unfortunately, no one was willing to cooperate, since at that time the notion of childhood depression seemed preposterous.

Soon afterward, McKnew accepted a staff appointment at Children's Hospital in Washington, D.C., where he met Cytryn. The two discussed their experiences with the "alleged" childhood depression, and immediately began to collaborate in studying the subject. That collaboration has lasted almost thirty years and still continues. Gradually, other child psychiatrists and members of other medical specialties have become interested, and today childhood depression is a widely recognized condition. There are official criteria for diagnosing this disorder, as well as a variety of drugs for use along with psychotherapy in treating it.

Adult Depression: An Ancient Malady

Depression is certainly the most widespread mental and emotional disorder afflicting humankind, and very probably the oldest. In ancient days it harassed Job, that wealthy, God-fearing Old Testament character who—at the instigation of Satan—is suddenly stricken by a succession of calamities. Enemies kill his herdsmen and drive off his cattle; fire from the skies burns up his thousands of sheep and his shepherds; marauders kill his camel drivers and drive off the camels; a whirlwind strikes the home of one of his sons and kills all ten of Job's children. Satan had predicted that when Job had thus been ruined he would curse the Lord. But Job says only, "The Lord gave, and the Lord hath taken away; blessed be the name of the Lord." Then Satan, having received the Lord's permission to strike at the man himself, afflicts Job with sores from head to foot. At this point Job's wife advises him to "curse God and die." Job answers, "Shall we receive good at the hand of God, and shall we not receive evil?" To friends who argue that he is being punished for his sins, he declares his innocence. Society despises him. Finally, he is driven to deny that God is just. Distraught and deeply depressed, he longs for death. As the story so vividly portrays, Job wards off feelings of despair over his numerous afflictions for a long period of time. However, he finally succumbs and displays symptoms of what we would now label as reactive depression.

Undoubtedly, depression has afflicted people for many thousands of years. It was the only recognized mental illness in antiquity and its description in the writings of Hippocrates and Galen, the leading physicians of ancient Greece and Rome, respectively, rivals any modern description in clarity and perceptiveness. Today it is found in all countries and cultures. In one way or another it has affected Abraham Lincoln, Winston Churchill, Theodore Roosevelt, Honoré de Balzac, Vincent van Gogh, Ernest Hemingway, and many others. In the United States the lifetime prevalence of just one type of depressive illness, namely major depressive disorder, is 8.7 percent for women and 3.6 percent for men.[4]

Despite its ancient history and universal range, depression in its various forms has until recently remained a mysterious malady whose causes could only be guessed at and whose treatment was largely guesswork. During the last thirty years, however, medical scientists have begun to answer many important questions surrounding it. Most importantly, they have learned in the great majority of cases to treat it effectively. During this same period, child psychiatrists have discovered that children are common victims of depression. To parents, teachers, physicians, counselors, and all other persons concerned with the welfare of the family, this is a finding of tremendous importance. A depressed child often goes undiagnosed or misdiagnosed, often seen as simply having a behavior problem. Though childhood depression is harder than adult depression to diagnose, it can be treated effectively. And there are indications that if treatment begins early the lifetime course of the disease may be ameliorated.

A Depressed Boy Tells His Story

The following is a slightly condensed interview conducted by one of us with a boy of high-school age who had a major depressive disorder.* The questions, put by Dr. McKnew, are answered directly by the boy, who comes from middle-class family.

What does your depression feel like today?

It's a coming-and-going thing. I don't feel depressed all the time. Usually it takes something, no matter how minor, to really set it off, and I start feeling bad about something and I can't do anything, and so today everything's been going pretty well, so I don't feel bad at all. But on another day, you know, I might just not want to get up in the morning or do anything at all.

Can you tell me more about it? What else do you feel?

Just like everything's worthless, like it's just not worth it to even be. That's about the best I can do. It's—it seems like it's a silly thing to even go through life and exist. And from one day to the next you're always wondering if you're going to make it to the next day if it's—if you can stand it, if it's worth trying to get to tomorrow. And—

Can you tell me what the hurt feels like a little bit?

Ah—not really. It's just—just, I feel like—I feel mostly like I'm worthless, like there's something wrong with me. It's really not a pleasant feeling to know that you're a total failure, a complete nothing, and I get the feeling that I didn't do nothing right or worthwhile or anything. Just—

Does it make you feel hopeless about life?

Yes. That's a very good way to describe it. . . .

Off and on, how long have you had some of these feelings? Can you date it back?

. . . I really started having problems like with school and things when I was in—well, that was about two years ago. Then before that, I really was hating school and missed, was absent, an awful lot. But I was always able to return and get back into things. And my grades really started to slip, and before that, I just plain old didn't like school. I had trouble making myself go all the time. But I've always done really well in school. It's not a

* American Broadcasting Companies, Inc. 1981. Reprinted by permission of ABC News.

matter of having trouble with getting the grades or anything like that. It was just a matter of hating it, getting up in the morning—

No pleasure?

That's probably the worst. Yeah. And I never really got along with other people at school that well—at least not since elementary school. So I'd have to say it started about sixth grade or, you know, maybe five, six years ago that I really started getting down. . . .

Even before that?

Yeah. Just—well, I've always—everyone tells me, anyway, that I've been a perfectionist. I don't even know exactly what that means, but I know that I was never doing things well enough to suit myself since—well, ever since I can remember. It's—nothing's ever been quite good enough. And then it kind of snowballed, and I got—it got so nothing was even good. And then everything was bad that I did, and then everything's terrible, and—

Yeah. And these last two years with school, sort of was—it progressed? To just not being able to go at all?

Yeah. I just—I got to hating school so much and hating my life in general. I was really getting to be a bore, and didn't like it, and one morning the alarm went off and I was lying there in bed and saying, "I have to get up to go to school . . . but I—I can't. I don't know what I'm going to do. I just can't get up." I couldn't do it. I couldn't make myself get up and get ready for school. No matter what—I just sat there and thought to myself, "What am I going to do?"—you know, and my whole life flashed before my eyes, and, you know, everything's going wrong and it felt like the end of the world, that I just couldn't do anything.

And then that continued on for days, and my mother would come in and say, you know—"Are you getting up for school today?" And I wouldn't say anything, because I didn't want to say, "No, I don't want to go to school," because it wasn't true. I wanted to be able to go to school and just go and get it over with, but I couldn't say, "Yes, I'm going," 'cause I knew I wasn't deep down inside. I knew there was no way I was going to school that day.

When you've really gotten as down as you can get, you've told me in the past you've thought about hurting yourself. Could you describe some of that?

I'm really afraid of pain, so it's not so much a matter of hurting myself. I just wish I wasn't what I was at all. I wish I wasn't alive. I wish there was some way I could just disappear off the face of the earth, never have been born or something along that line. If you're asking me did suicide come up, yeah, a lot. That was in my mind an awful lot. But I—

But you hate pain—

Yeah, that's right. Well, let's see—the best way I could think of was a drug overdose or something like that. That was all I could really think of, because—well, I couldn't blow my brains out—I didn't have a pistol or anything like that. That was for sure. And besides, that would hurt. There wasn't really much to it. I just—I'd think, "Boy, I wish I was dead," and then I'd think, "That's ridiculous," you know, " 'cause you're never going to be able to kill yourself. You don't have enough guts for that."

You're a flop at suicide, too.

Yeah. Right. That entered my mind—

Good Lord. Isn't that something. Now there've been a lot of efforts to try to do something to make it better for you. You came to see me a little over a year ago. What seems to get in the way of getting some help for you?

Well, children—well, I guess I should say adolescents—aren't real people at all in this world. You know, they don't have real, live emotions or feelings. They can't think; they can't do; they're possessions and they kind of exist. And so no one has really even thought about, you know, what's wrong with the kid. You know, it's just—it was a matter of, well, he'll either "grow out of it" or something like this. You know, "If we just talk to him for a while," you know. "It's obvious that he's just not being logical about anything." Which was—couldn't be further from the truth.

You mean your feelings weren't taken seriously?

Yeah.

What you felt was a bunch of baloney 'cause you're just a kid and can't feel—

Yeah. I was just being dumb or trying to get attention or something like that, you know. So I went to a few counselors and things, and they told me that, you know, that I would have to set goals in my life and, you know, that I would have to want to go to school . . . like—well, "Next week, what you're going to have to do is, say, you're going to have to make up your mind to go to school and then go and just do it." Or I'd get a lot of advice like, "You don't have to be an all-A student or anything. Just get through it. Just go, do the least amount you can do, and—" But that's impossible—at least for me. . . .

Yeah. And what happened to the idea of trying to get some medicine that might make you—?

Ah, yeah. I finally got on an antidepressant from my family doctor, who I guess would probably be one of the wisest people I've ever met. He's really, really nice and smart, and I liked him a lot. . . . When I finally went back to a psychiatrist, he said that—he told my Mom that it was—that it was okay if I wanted to get off of it, to discontinue it. And which I did, because I felt kind of bad about being dependent on this stuff to be able to get up in the morning and to function.

Although it was helping you.

Yeah. I—it must have, because I was able to go back to school, at least temporarily. But it had side effects and stuff, and I didn't like it, so I decided to get off of it. I was going to, and the psychiatrist told my Mom that it was okay that I should get off. So I got off and got really depressed and quit school again, and it all went back to the way it was before.

If you could tell us what a day in your life feels like right now—I know we've talked about it, but if you could do it again it would be very helpful.

Well, okay. It would—I—first of all, I'd stay up really late worrying about the next day. Okay. And that would turn into the day. It would go past one or two, 'cause when I get depressed, I don't sleep at all. And I'd really start worrying about the next day—I'm—and what I'm going to do when my mother comes in and asks me whether I'm going to school or not, and, you know, what's going to happen when I don't do anything. So it comes time in the morning, and my Mom comes in and gets me up, and asks me if I'm going to school, and I don't say anything. I just bury myself as far into the pillows as I can, and she leaves, being rather upset and miserable about the whole thing. Okay.

So I lay in bed, and if I can go back to sleep, great, 'cause then that's kind of an escape for, what, another two hours? I don't have to exist [*laughs*]. I don't have to worry about anything or anything like that. So—but if I can't, then I just start thinking about how lousy everything is going for me. Here I am lying in bed doing absolutely nothing all day. I'm not a—I'm not a sitter. I don't sit back and watch things happen. I—I—I do all right. I go after things that I want—usually. But this depression just absolutely incapacitates me. I can't do anything. I can't do anything I want to do; I can't do anything I don't want to do. I can't make myself do anything. . . . I don't even get up to eat. The only time I can eat is when everyone's gone to bed, because then I don't have to look 'em in the face or see 'em at all. 'Cause I feel really bad about not having done what I was supposed to do for that day, you know. Especially as a child, there are certain things you're expected to do day in and day out, each day. You're supposed to go to school, you're not supposed to skip classes or anything— blah, blah, blah, blah, etcetera [*sighing*]. And—and I don't do any of these things that I'm supposed to do—at all—when I get depressed. And that makes it worse, 'cause I feel bad about not doing the things I was supposed to do.

And tell me again a little bit about the pain that this then makes you feel.

Well, I suppose most people don't have something—well, I don't know—this—it's something that you hate so intensely that, well, if you can't forget it, you just have to try to push it out of your mind, 'cause it—it'll tear you right up. There's nothing you can do—just sit there and mumble to yourself over and over again, "Oh, I hate myself," and, you know, "I hate you," talking to yourself. . . .

And do you feel sort of empty and—and devoid of any sense of purpose or—?

Well, not an empty kind of feeling, but just like you're full, you're full of nothing. I've—you've—you've got this fantastic ability to do wrong and bad, and stuff—

Oh. So you're full of bad feelings rather than just devoid of—

Yeah. And you feel really alone because no one understands—at all. Totally—you know. I even talked to kids my age, and they say, "Yeah, I know how you feel. I really hate school too." But if they did [*laughing*] they wouldn't go. I—I found that out pretty quickly. If you hate something that bad. . . .

You take any pleasure in—in anything?

Yeah. I like music a lot—I played in the band and sang in choir at school—and theater and the people. I like people a lot. I like being around 'em as much as possible. . . .

When you do those things, do you come up a little bit?

Yeah. You forget. If you get busy enough, you forget what's going on. You forget that you don't feel bad—it sounds kind of silly, but you think if you could forget that you don't feel bad, then you don't but you—you still do. You feel terrible. And then if something goes wrong while you're doing something fun, like you make a mistake or something, oh, you just—you feel like "Well, that's it. I'm—even at something I enjoy doing I'm no good." You just kind of feel like giving up. . . .

[*To the boy's mother*] *I was wondering if you might share with us some of how you viewed your son's adventure through the land of depression.*

[Mother] Well, it was a very difficult—I didn't realize he was having problems with depression at a young age. He—the school thing was like he did very well at the beginning, and then it—it would drop off as it went along. But two years ago, he had a viral infection, and they thought it was mononucleosis. And I took him to a doctor, and he was sure it was, so he told me to keep him out of school, because this is a long kind of disease, and so I did. . . . By the time we found that it wasn't mono, he had missed like a semester of school. He kept saying he was so depressed at this time, during the time when he—we thought he had mono.

And I read books and stuff, and it says that viral infections sometimes will bring on a depression. So I went to my family doctor, and I told him that my son was very depressed. And he said—this is not the same family doctor we'd been to talk with before—he said, "What's he got to be depressed about? You know, after all, he's just a kid. Why should he be depressed?"

These last sentences show how many clinicians felt and acted when confronted with cases of childhood depression a decade ago—and still too often do: "After all, he's just a kid. Why should he be depressed?" As we go along, we'll discuss many reasons why even "just a kid" becomes depressed.

Cases like the foregoing one still go unrecognized year after year, despite the greater public recognition of childhood depression.

Depression among Children

Because of our professional experiences, we have been interested in all aspects of childhood depression: its etiology, recognition, treatment, and prevention. We have studied and treated children from all social classes. No matter what the family environment was like, the basic symptoms of depression were the same from child to child.

In one of our first studies we looked at a group of children, each of whom had a close relative who had been hospitalized for treatment of a major depressive illness.[5] One girl, a worried looking ten-year-old, told us: "I am the biggest troublemaker in our family. I cry a lot and feel weird a lot." Speaking in a tense, slow voice—a monotone—she added that she doesn't sleep well, feels ugly, and has thought of suicide. She joked about jumping out of the window. Then she mentioned some recent dreams. In one of them she leaves the house and, when she tries to return, cannot find it. In another she runs away and injures her foot.

A twelve-year-old boy was sad, tense, and fidgety. In a low voice, and between spells of crying, he told us that he feels sad, lonely, and inferior. "I think I am the stupidest kid in class," he said. "I never really try to kill myself, but sometimes I think to drown myself." He drew a plane and said: "It will kill people on the beach."

A girl of eleven was relaxed, showed only occasional signs of sadness, and spoke softly. She stays alone much of the time, she said, and cries sometimes when criticized. She told about her dreams. In one series she is in a maze and dogs are chasing her; she is caught by a man with a gun, hurts her leg, and can't get up. In another series, a girl dies, a boy runs away from his stepfather, and King Arthur's kingdom is destroyed.

Although none of the children who had a depressed close relative was psychotic or insane, most scored higher than average on rating scales for childhood depression. The children were as young as four and as old as fifteen. More than 50 percent of them, it turned out, were clearly depressed.

Among all children in the United States, the percentage with significant symptoms of depression is much lower (though still much higher than anyone imagined twenty years ago). Our studies, some of which will be discussed later, indicate that the incidence of all types of depressive disorders in children ranges from 5 percent to 10 percent. The prevalence of major depressive disorder in this age group approaches 3 percent and more than doubles in adolescence.[6]

The Nicest Kid on the Block

Why had depression in children gone unrecognized for so long? For thousands of years adults have been known to be afflicted by it; for thousands of years physicians and others have written about its occurrence in adults. Yet its presence in children was missed until twenty-five or so years ago. From our experience, perhaps the biggest reason is that many depressed children are often the "nicest" boys and girls on the block and the best behaved kids in school. Go into a classroom and you'll find that the kids in the back rows are often the quiet ones, the ones who don't give anyone any trouble. We know now that many of them may be depressed. They're often well mannered and shy, and they seem to like to help people. The mischief makers, the kids with behavior disorders—they're up front where the teacher can easily keep an eye on them. A parallel situation exists on most pediatric wards, where the depressed children are usually found tucked away in the corner far from the nurses station. The nurses are often unaware of the difficulty because of the children's "nice" behavior and the fact that they don't give anybody trouble.

As a matter of fact, many depressed adults are like these well-behaved children. Some of them are the nicest people, the most thoughtful, the hardest working. Often the thing a psychiatrist has to do is to get them to look out for their own needs and welfare and not go on trying to take care of everybody else.

Unless you know a depressed child quite well and are really looking for signs of depression, you probably won't notice anything wrong. But if you ask him, "How are you really feeling today?" he'll probably answer, "I feel awful," or, as the adolescent said in the previous interview, "You just kind of feel like giving up. . . ."

What makes many depressed children and adults seems uncomplaining and so eager to help others? We suspect that an important part of the answer to this question lies in a poor self-image and a deep-seated conflict over the handling of hostile and angry feelings. The fear that angry feelings may be potentially harmful to oneself or to others may teach a depressed person to avoid or even suppress such feelings at any cost. Unfortunately, the price exacted by the process may be extremely high in terms of personal suffering.

In the beginning of this chapter, in describing Leon Cytryn's findings of depressive symptoms in children with chronic illness and handicaps, we alluded to the fact that children with congenital amputation have been surprisingly free of emotional disturbance. This finding has been confirmed by researchers in Canada, England, and Germany.[3] When we investigated this phenomenon, we discovered that these children shared a remarkable freedom, fostered by their parents and caretakers, to express their aggression openly. Such an externalization of aggression seemed to have been a protection against the development of depressive symptoms seen in most severely handicapped children. This crucial relationship between depression and aggression will be elaborated in subsequent chapters.

What Is Childhood Depression?

Depression is a state that is common to all mankind. It is marked by sadness, a feeling of worthlessness, and a conviction that nothing one can do matters. Under many circumstances, depression may be quite appropriate—for example, when a loved one dies or when a person suffers other losses, real or imagined. If a friend leaves town, if you move to another neighborhood, if your children have to change schools—all these and many other circumstances may give you the blues and leave you feeling low and depressed for days and even weeks. Each of us experiences this type of depression at one time or another. We are not clinically depressed but in a depressed mood.

However, there is a point at which such a response to loss and other sources of stress stops being appropriate and becomes a type of mental illness. This chapter is devoted in large part to describing how we know when a child is nearing the danger point, how we can prevent him or her from reaching it, and how we can restore to health a child with a depressive disorder.

Differences between Mood or Affect and Disorder

Parents often ask how to distinguish between a depressed mood or affect and a depressive disorder. One way is to notice the duration and intensity of the condition. A child who shows no signs of being comforted or of resuming a normal life within a week after falling into a low mood (for whatever reason)—or within six months after undergoing what is to him a severe loss—is at risk of developing a depressive disorder.

Another measure is the ability of the stricken child to function in everyday life. Does the child play as much as usual? Keep up with his or her class in school? Perform work adequately? Engage in the usual activities? If the child's functioning continues to deteriorate, we may be dealing with a more serious disorder which needs prompt attention.

Sudden changes in eating and sleeping patterns can be an indicator, too. Appetite often either falls off or increases with the start of a depressive disorder. If it doesn't return to normal within a few weeks, the child needs help. The same is true of sleep problems. Among these are failure to fall asleep at the usual time, waking up during the night and having trouble getting back to sleep, and waking up in the morning unusually early. A depressed child may get a great deal of sleep and still feel constantly tired.

In some cases, the presence of suicidal tendencies is a giveaway. Some depressed children have suicidal thoughts. As their depression deepens, they may plan and even attempt suicide. Usually they keep the thoughts to themselves, but gentle probing can bring them out.

Most of us have heard or read a good deal about depressive disorders in adults but much less about such illness in children. Many of us know adults who are depressed. Children often do not show their depression so openly; they do not wear it on their sleeve, as adults may do. Children tend to be depressed in an extremely quiet way. They often creep off to their rooms or other secluded places and cry while appearing cheerful in public settings. Usually they don't look as sad, tearful, or slowed down as depressed adults. By the time a child exhibits signs of depression for all to see, he or she usually is *severely* depressed. The level of depression that is obvious in an adult often goes unrecognized in children by teachers, parents, and even friends.

For some of us, a more powerful reason than the above for the difference in visibility between childhood and adult depression is the way we view childhood. Looking back on it, we tend to view childhood as a happy time, though many children do not look on it that way, and though Charles Dickens and other perceptive novelists certainly have not. Recalling our own childhood through the rainbow-colored mists of time, many of us see the early years as a period during which one could not possibly be depressed, except momentarily.

Depression in Adults

Beyond the bouts of temporary depressive moods that most of us experience at one time or another and usually pull through on our own, there are two serious types of adult depression. The *unipolar* patient is at the depressive end of the mood spectrum, while the *bipolar* may exhibit symptoms at both ends of the spectrum.

An adult with the unipolar mood disorder is depressed for a significant period of time, usually six to nine months. No matter how hard he tries, he cannot find happiness either in work or in recreation. He is acutely dispirited. A former patient has written that he lived "in a world in which the sun had gone down and never come up again, in which fear was the dominant emotion, a world in which there was no joy." Many times the unipolar adult is listless, finds it very hard or even impossible to go about his work and other customary activities, and may think about or attempt to commit suicide. Sometimes, however, unipolar illness may induce many depressive symptoms without seriously interfering with work. It will probably interfere more with the individual's family or social life, both because he lacks energy and because he is not a companionable person to be around.

Two famous examples of depressed adults are Abraham Lincoln and Winston Churchill. Both men accomplished prodigious amounts of brilliant work while suffering from intermittent bouts of serious depression, a state which Churchill used to call "the black dog."

The adult with bipolar illness is sad and dispirited when he reaches the depressed end of the spectrum, agitated and excited when he reaches the manic end. Such a person is often referred to as *manic-depressive*. During the manic period he may feel unusually well and strong, go without sleep for long periods, and, because he feels like Superman, plunge into vast, foolish undertakings in his personal or business affairs. Psychiatrist Nathan Kline,[1] an authority on depressive disorders, told about a man from a very wealthy family who had been treated for depression and suddenly became manic, telephoned his brokers, and placed orders for almost half a million dollars worth of stocks. Kline told also of a woman patient who went into a department store to buy some dish towels and ended up spending six thousand dollars. At the opposite or depression end, said Kline, "aggressive action is replaced by extreme withdrawal, chronic excitement gives way to listless torpor, and in extreme cases the patient becomes unable to manage the simplest matters." When depressed, the bipolar person may attempt suicide.

Unipolar and bipolar illnesses are thought to be hereditary, usually cause some degree of incapacitation, and sometimes occur in psychotic form. The majority of adults with mood disorders, however, has a different form of depression, called *minor* or *dysthymic*. This disorder is generally characterized by less acute impairment, fewer symptoms, and absence of psychosis; however, frequently its course is protracted. In fact, one of the most difficult cases of mood disorders involves a so-called "double depression," a term coined by well-known researcher Hagop Akiskal. In this disorder, an episode of major depression overlies a chronic dysthymic disorder.

Classification of Depression in Children: Historical Perspective

Childhood depression has been generally recognized as a distinct illness for over twenty years. Before that, as pointed out in Chapter One, it had been ignored or treated as a behavior disorder. One of the first to classify it was Warren A. Weinberg, who with colleagues at Washington University in St. Louis drew up a set of criteria in the early 1970s.[2]

These criteria or benchmarks for depression were that the child show both an unhappy mood and a sense of self-depreciation, and two or more of the following symptoms: aggressive behavior, sleep disturbance, lessened desire to socialize with people, change in attitude toward school, change in school performance, physical complaints, loss of usual energy, and unusual change in appetite or weight or both. The symptoms had to be different from the child's usual behavior, and they had to continue for at least one month.

About twenty-five years ago we proposed a classification that described three types of depression in school-age children or children from six to twelve. Under our classification, childhood depression was divided among three main types—acute, chronic, and masked.[3]

The acute and chronic types have similar features. These include severe impairment of the child's scholastic and social adjustment; disturbances of sleep and eating; feelings of despair, helplessness, and hopelessness; retardation of movement; and occasional suicidal thoughts or attempts. The main difference between these two types lies in precipitating causes, the child's adjustment before illness, the length of the illness, and the family history. Children with chronic depression, in contrast to those with the acute type, do not always have a known immediate precipitating cause, their illness lasts longer, and there is a history of marginal social and emotional adjustment, of previous depressive episodes, and of depressive illness in close family members, particularly the mother.

Children with the acute type of depression seem to fall ill in response to some traumatic event in their lives or the lives of those close to them. Mother has had to go to the hospital, Grandpa has died, the family has moved, an especially favorite toy has disappeared—all these and many similar occurrences may precipitate an acute attack.

The distinction between acute and chronic depression flowed in large part from our early observation and treatment of children ill enough to be hospitalized. In later years our experience has increasingly widened to include outpatients, that is, children who do not have to be hospitalized but are treated instead in a clinic or doctor's office.

In children with the type of disorder called masked depression, the sickness is very often associated with so-called acting-out behavior. This arises when a person tries to relieve or act out an emotional problem through such antisocial acts as stealing, setting fires, using drugs, running away, and beating up people, which bring on a host of related problems. Parents or others may sum up such activities by saying the child is "being bad" or has a "behavior problem."

The first two categories (chronic and acute) have remained operationally valid and been useful in our research and clinical work. However, masked depressive reaction has proved a difficult and controversial clinical entity. Almost all who have studied depressed children find severe depression very frequently associated with aggressive and somatic symptoms. If the acting-out behavior predominates and the depression seems secondary and of less magnitude in the clinical picture, the child should properly be diagnosed as having, say, a conduct disturbance with depressive features. On the other hand, if the child fits the established criteria for a depressive disorder, that should be the primary diagnosis, with other diagnostic features stated as ancillary. In such a way the acting-out symptoms frequently will become an integral part of the depressive picture rather than a mask.[4]

As an example of the chronic type, consider the case of seven-year-old Christine, who couldn't sleep well, ate little, and had episodes of screaming. She often threatened suicide because she thought of herself as "a bad girl" and felt that nobody loved her. The girl's mother was a helpless woman overwhelmed by family responsibilities, poor self-esteem, and a tendency toward frequent depressions. Christine had been born out of wedlock and her stepfather had spanked the girl frequently. The trouble may have started many years earlier; Christine's mother had been neglected by her own mother and brought up in an atmosphere of hostility.

One of the most important persons in Christine's life had

been the paternal grandmother, who cared for her during infancy. Suddenly, though, when the girl was a year old, her chief care was shifted to a maternal aunt. The mother herself left Christine for several months when the girl was one and a half years old and again when she was four. Continuity of loving care makes for a stronger emotional life, and this girl had had little of it.

Six-year-old Barbara is a child who suffered the acute type of childhood depression. In her case the precipitating cause was the mugging of an older sister, 17, who had been serving as the girl's surrogate mother while the real mother worked fulltime outside the home. After the mugging, the sister became withdrawn and less attentive. Within three months Barbara was admitted to a psychiatric ward because she had gradually dropped her usual activities, slept poorly, lacked appetite, and was failing school. Evidence that she was markedly depressed could be found in her sad and tearful facial expression, her monotonous voice, words indicating hopelessness and despair, and slowness of movement.

After several days of hospital care and attention, but with no specific treatment for depression, the girl became outgoing and began to eat and sleep regularly. Her mood brightened and she was sociable, active, and alert. Two years later the mother reported that Barbara was maintaining her gains.

What we once called masked depression is illustrated by Albert, a twelve-year-old sent to us because of his disruptive behavior in school. He was hyperactive and aggressive; his grades were poor and his social adjustment marginal. A look at the home situation revealed a mother who worked away from home fulltime and was unable either to provide adequate care for Albert or to find a mother-substitute, and an alcoholic father who assumed no responsibility for the family and who often beat Albert. Like many others with a similar condition, the boy had experienced both rejection and depreciation.

Throughout our interview with him, Albert was apathetic and sad. He described himself as dumb and expressed the belief that everyone was picking on him. He saw himself as helpless.

When he fantasized, he showed a strong interest in themes of annihilation, violence, explosions, and death—invariably with a bad outcome for the main figures. The authors believe that the boy's delinquency and aggressiveness were attempts to escape from a basic depression. While such a defense is self-destructive, it does help ward off the unbearable feeling of despair.

Albert did not improve. In fact, a year and a half later he was sent to a residential school for delinquent boys. The management of Albert's case was poor. Under the best circumstances he would have been sent to a good psychiatric facility with therapists to work with him and with his family. With excellent care, some delinquent children are able to do remarkably well. The tragedy is that, while depressed delinquents need much more care than the average depressed child, such care is not usually available. There are just not enough workers in the field who are both interested in providing such care and know how to give it. So the Alberts in this world, who need the most care, usually get the least and end up in homes for delinquents, where the outlook for the rest of their lives is bleak. They continue to live on the fringe of society and, all too often, go on to become hardened criminals.

Different Manifestations of Depression

The depressive process in children manifests itself at several different levels.[5] The deepest level is *unconscious,* so named because the child is not consciously aware of the real meaning of what is running through his mind or motivates his behavior. He may dream, for instance, that he is being chased by a ferocious dog, cannot get away, and may wake up screaming.

There are many ways besides dreams by which an expert can get a glimpse of what's really on a child's mind. The way a child reacts to part of a television program, or a movie, or a book, or the kind of story he tells to go along with a picture he has drawn may reveal what is bothering the child unconsciously. There are even tests specifically designed to "tap" the unconscious. One, the Thematic Apperception Test, is a series of pictures on cards.

The child tells a story about what he sees in the pictures and in the telling often reveals his worries and concerns. Another test is the Rorschach, in which the child is shown a series of ink blots and asked to tell what he sees in each one. Depressive themes, as they emerge in these tests, include mistreatment, criticism, abandonment, personal injury, death, and suicide.

Another way in which the depressive process may show itself is *verbal expression*. Whether talking or writing spontaneously or responding to questions, the child reveals that she feels hopeless, helpless, worthless, unattractive, unloved, and guilty, and that suicidal ideas keep running through her mind. When asked, the child will describe her depressed feelings just as clearly as an adult. She will talk about feeling sad or blue or hopeless or about being unable to get out of bed or about not wanting to do anything.

Yet another way the depressive process may make itself known is through *mood* and *behavior*. Here there is no need for talking: an observer can see for himself, just by watching the child, that something is wrong. Signs include sadness of facial expression and posture, crying, slowness of movement and emotional reactions, disturbances of appetite and sleep, school failure, physical complaints for which no physical cause can be found, and sometimes irritability.

Interestingly, when the depressive symptoms begin to fade, the signs included under mood and behavior go first. These are the more superficial symptoms and the ones at the conscious level. This is usually followed by the disappearance of depression as it is expressed verbally. Such expression is at a deeper, preconscious level. The material expressed unconsciously is the last to disappear, usually only after the depressive problem has been cleared up. This material lies at the deepest level. Thus, the disappearance of symptoms in depression follows a hierarchical order known since the time of Freud.

Using Defenses against Depression

Since depressive feelings are emotionally painful, children—and adults—often seek to avoid experiencing and expressing them. For example, here is young Bill, who has just lost a part-time job he had expected would keep him in pocket money until he graduated from high school two years hence. As frequently happens with Bill when experiencing a disappointment, he begins to feel depressed. But he pushes this feeling aside and goes into action. He asks his friends if they know of a job, he seeks advice from his guidance counselor, he canvasses the businesses and factories in town. Unaware that he is doing so, Bill is using the most effective type of defense: *sublimation*. Instead of moping around the house and feeling lower and lower, he is translating his concern into high-level action. Put another way, he is handling depressive feelings by diverting them into channels of which other people—and he himself—approve. But there are many others, which Anna Freud, daughter of the founder of psychoanalysis, outlined in her book *The Ego and the Mechanisms of Defense.*[6]

One of the most primitive and potentially dangerous defense techniques is *denial:* the depressed child simply refuses to acknowledge thoughts or feelings that are too painful. A classic example of denial is the diabetic child who will not take her insulin because she refuses to acknowledge that she has a serious physical illness. Many such children actually die because they will not use their medicine. The same is true of adults with heart disease. Denying that they have an ailment needing treatment and rest, they refuse treatment and go back to work too soon.

Projection is another destructive defense. Here, something that the depressed child cannot accept in himself is projected onto—or attributed to—others. The child or adult may feel that he doesn't like somebody, but this feeling is unacceptable to him. It's easier to think that the other person doesn't like *him.* What he is actually doing is projecting his own feelings onto the other person.

The most common example of projection is prejudice. In an

effort not to feel inferior themselves, many people ascribe inferiority to whole groups of other people—for instance, African-Americans, Jews, and certain nationalities. In other words, they project their own feelings of inferiority onto other people and act accordingly; they cannot face up to their own sense of inadequacy, so they find it elsewhere. Projection can become the basis for a paranoid view of life. People who use it a great deal go around thinking everybody's out to get them. They are less likely to be overtly depressed than people who use other types of defense.

In *acting out,* another type of defense, a person temporarily suppresses her depression by engaging in antisocial behavior. This may range from cheating on a test or swiping a little money from parents to setting fires or killing someone. Albert, the previously described delinquent, could be a good example of a user of this defense.

Another commonly employed defense is *dissociation of affect.* Here a child unconsciously represses his depressive feelings while retaining a memory of the event that evoked these feelings. Such a defense mechanism often operates after a serious loss. The child may talk matter-of-factly about an event such as death of a parent while continuing to play without any visible sign of unhappiness. Such behavior, if not understood, will appear callous to an adult and, in fact, has been used in the past as one argument against the existence of childhood depression.

Dissociation of affect is a mild form of the dissociation phenomenon. In more severe forms both the affect and the stressful memory become unconscious and give rise to a whole group of dissociative disorders, such as some forms of post-traumatic stress disorder and multiple personality disorder. Interestingly, dissociative disorders are usually accompanied by prominent depressive features.

Reaction formation is another commonly employed defense. Here the person talks or behaves contrary to the way she really feels. For instance, a child may dislike or even hate one of his parents. Since such feelings may be intolerable for a child with high standards, she unconsciously converts hate into love and exhibits overly friendly behavior toward the parent. Reaction formation sometimes seems like sublimation, but unlike sublimation it provides no pleasure and no long-term solutions.

Another common mental mechanism frequently seen in people with affective illness is *introjection*. This is the opposite of projection. The introjective type of person feels that everything is his own fault, even when people are treating him badly. He turns the natural dislike and hatred that he feels inward. While the previously discussed defenses either ward off depression or mitigate its damage, introjection usually fosters depressive feelings and may often be a precipitant of the disorder itself.

All these defenses are used at all three levels of the depressive process described in the preceding section, that is, unconscious, verbal, and mood and behavior. At each level, the defenses have various degrees of efficiency; they do not always succeed in relieving a person of his or her depressive feelings. The extent to which the defenses work depends both on the severity of the problem the child faces and the state of her psychological or biological processes.

Maturation

In infancy the child has available only a limited number of defense mechanisms. The unconscious is primitive and does not always enable him either to contain his depressive emotions or to get rid of them. Moreover, since the infant cannot use words, he is unable to talk out depressive feelings or seek solutions to situations that induce such feelings. Unable to assess his life situation, the infant is not psychologically equipped to develop a depressive disorder as we know it in adults, which involves not only sad affect but a sense of rejection and a negative valuation of one's life situation. However, when stress (primarily loss of love objects) is overwhelming and of long duration, the infant may develop a primitive depressive state characterized by a sad face, withdrawal, failure to interact, and even refusal of food. Such primitive depressive states will be described in Chapter Three, where we discuss the work of Spitz, Bowlby, and Mahler on infant depression.

Even under overwhelming circumstances of deprivation and neglect, the infant's push for maturation and the ability to substitute for losses help to counteract the depressive process—unless the child is genetically vulnerable to depression. This may explain why depression in infants is often short-lived except in situations, such as the ones existing in some hospitals and other institutions, where substitutes for losses of loved persons or things cannot be found.

The toddler's growth promotes a sense of optimism, exuberance, and hope that helps ward off the sense of despair or hopelessness. Expressed another way, the push for physical growth has its counterpart in psychological mechanisms that help prevent or counteract depression.

When a loss has occurred, the toddler has a greater ability than does an adult to substitute a variety of love objects, which may be persons, places, or things, for what has been lost. This ability can lessen the impact of loss. Further, the child has a less developed ability to test reality, or to tell whether or not a given emotion or circumstance is indeed real. As a result, he or she can more readily use developing defense mechanisms to ward off the perception of loss. For instance, if a well-loved possession has been destroyed, the child, using the defense of denial, may insist that it merely has been left somewhere. Finally, the conscience of the young child is less developed than that of older children and adults. Therefore, the feelings of guilt and lowered self-esteem that may form the basis of depressive states at older age levels tend, in toddlerhood, to be less severe. During this period, we seldom see a clearly delineated depressive syndrome but rather a variety of behavioral deviations. These deviations probably represent precursors of a variety of psychiatric disorders in childhood. As will be discussed in Chapter Three, our studies and those of our colleagues give us a glimpse as to how this matrix of behavioral deviations crystallizes into the various distinct disorders clearly diagnosable in later childhood.

In five-to-six-year-old children, we begin to be able to make a diagnosis of specific depressive disorders. We attribute this to the following developmental factors. Increased intellectual development allows children to assess more properly past and future events. Attachment to a parental figure should have helped them achieve a reasonable degree of object stability. In addition, language development permits the child to clearly describe his feeling states.

In addition, a number of children from five to twelve years old, the period known to psychoanalysts as the latency stage, have to deal with an extremely harsh conscience, often because they have been raised by rigid or punitive or obsessional parents. A harsh conscience is the harsh parent or harsh school-teacher in the child's head saying, *"Do that right or I will punish you."* Some children, including a few even younger than five, incorporate such harshness into their thinking at an early age, which makes them vulnerable to depression.

One of McKnew's young patients provided a vivid example of introjection by saying one day, "You know, I think I have a mother in my head." This mother in the girl's head would tell her to do this and that, and when she couldn't live up to the mother's expectations she would become depressed. Not until adolescence, when they are better able to discern the real from the unreal world, and to test reality better, do such children soften their conscience.

With the advent of adolescence, the balance of forces bearing on growth shifts to favor a breakthrough of the depressive process into words and into openly depressive mood and behavior. The growth process, which worked against depressive feelings earlier, gradually diminishes in late adolescence. Substitution for lost loved ones becomes increasingly difficult. The process of testing reality is maturing, so the tendency to use fantasy as an escape is counteracted, and more primitive defenses, like denial, are not as readily available.

Opposing these factors that favor the emergence of depression are more mature defenses, primarily sublimation. Other favorable factors are the ability to put one's feelings spontaneously into words and an increased capacity to solve problems.

The APA's Classification of Depression

Adult depression has been classified by the American Psychiatric Association (APA), and the results appear in the current edition of the *Diagnostic and Statistical Manual of Mental Disorders.* The current version of this manual is referred to as *DSM-IV,* the fourth edition.

We have made an item-for-item comparison among symptoms of childhood depression as proposed by various investigators and symptoms of adult depression as set forth in the current manual. As a result, we conclude that the criteria generally accepted for adults can also be used for children, as the APA suggests.

DSM-IV lists three kinds of depression:

1. Major Depressive Disorder, single episode. (This type corresponds to what we called acute depression.)
2. Major Depressive Disorder, recurrent.
3. Dysthymic Disorder. (The name dysthymic is derived from that of the thymus gland, which some investigators once mistakenly thought was concerned with a type of depression. The name itself does not tell anything about the kind of illness it designates.)

   (Both of these types correspond to the one we called chronic depression.)

There is no equivalent here for so-called masked depression. As we have treated more and more children and extended our research, we have realized that depression frequently occurs concomitantly with many other types of mental illness, such as conduct disorder and anxiety disorders, and that the depressive type we formerly called "masked" needs to be defined not so much as a distinct state, but as depression per se or as a subdiagnosis in other clinical disorders. To say that a child is masking depression, we conclude, there has to be real depression, verbally expressed, under the mask of delinquency and/or other behavioral problems.[4]

The *number* of children in the first two diagnoses, which cover major depressive illness, is quite large. In the United States it probably runs into the hundreds of thousands. Children with a major depressive illness represent approximately 1 percent of the population. However, most depressed children fall into the third APA class—dysthymic. In the 1980s Dr. Javad Kashani, the authors, and others conducted an epidemiological study in New Zealand of the frequency and type of depressive disorders in 650 normal nine-year-old children. The results were as follows: prevalence at the time of the study—major depression 1.7 percent, minor depression (dysthmic disorder) 3.6 percent. The past (up until nine years of age) prevalence in this group—major depression 1.0 percent, minor depression 8.5 percent.[7]

Indications of depressive illness, as listed in *DSM-IV,* include unhappiness, sadness, hopelessness, loss of appetite, disturbance of sleep, slowness of movement or agitation, loss of pleasure, loss of energy, low self-esteem, decreased concentration, and suicidal thoughts or actions. All of these may not be present in one person but at least five must be present for a diagnosis of major depression. In addition, a depressed child is likely to show disturbances in his or her school behavior. Other signs are feelings of guilt, loss of interest in life, complaints about physical illness, anxiety when separated from a loved person or thing or place, loneliness, restlessness, sulkiness, irritability, and feelings of helplessness.

In evaluating a child, in addition to looking at depressive symptoms and their time course, one has to examine the degree of functional impairment. If impairment is *mild,* symptoms result in only minor disturbance in school functioning or in usual activities and relationships with family or friends. If it is *severe,* symptoms markedly interfere with all usual activities, such as school functioning, social activities, or relationships with family or friends. *Moderate* impairment lies between the above. Some children develop delusions and hallucinations along with depressive symptoms; then the phrase *with psychotic features* is added to the diagnosis.

Wherever one looks in the history of medicine, one finds that the signs and symptoms of the illness we call depression are essentially the same. Nathan Kline says in his book *From Sad to Glad:*

> Depression is an ancient malady, one probably present at the dawn of history. It appears today in all societies from the most primitive to the most complex. . . . This is a natural illness, something inherent in the human condition, and not just a by-product of the anxieties created by modern times.[1]

Symptoms alone are usually not enough to reveal the type of depression from which the child is suffering or the most promising kind of treatment. What must be known in addition to the symptoms are the history of the illness and information about school, family, and friends. The situation is a little like that with a physical illness such as diabetes. If the child is known to have high blood sugar, the physician may diagnose it as a case of juvenile diabetes. But the physician wants to know more than that. He wants to know, for example, when the patient first became sick and what other symptoms he has, if these occur in connection with emotional upset, and if there is a family history of diabetes. Of course, at present we do not have a blood test for depression, which makes the history of the disorder all the more important.

Rarer Kinds of Childhood Affective Disorders

The kinds of depression described so far in this chapter are called *unipolar;* that means mood deviates toward the depression end of the continuum but it does not swing toward mania. These disorders are the ones most commonly found in children. But there are some other, less frequently encountered types, which are called *bipolar* disorders. They consist of some combination of depressive episodes as we have described above and periodic episodes of mania or hypomania, a mild version of mania. Manic episodes consist of distinct periods of elevated or irritable mood, lasting at least four days to one week. Accompanying symptoms are grandiosity, decreased need for sleep, pressure of speech, racing thoughts, distractibility, hyperactivity, poor judgment, and risky behaviors. Mania runs from minimal symptoms to symptoms requiring almost continual supervision to prevent physical harm to self or others, and can be accompanied by psychotic symptoms. Hypomania, on the other hand, never causes the degree of impairment seen in mania and is never accompanied by psychosis.

In children, the association of major depression and mania (also called *bipolar I disorder*) is extremely rare, while the *bipolar II disorder,* which is a combination of major depression and hypomania is more frequent, and is often preceded by an episode of major depression. Exact statistics on the prevalence of this disorder in children are unavailable, but one recent study reports that 31 percent of children treated for an episode of major depressive disorder developed a bipolar episode within several years of follow-up.[8]

Tom's case is typical of hypomania. He was eight years old when he sustained a severe electrical burn. His left forearm had to be amputated, and the upper half of his body was severely scarred. He spent a year on the surgical ward of a hospital, where his mood was generally one of elation. He was inappropriately jocular and extremely restless. He expressed grandiose ideas about his abilities, strength, and wealth but never had a complete break with reality. His hypomanic behavior increased at times of stress, such as just before an operation or when revealing his scarred body. Occasionally, there were brief periods of sadness, slowness of movement, and depression. Usually these were followed by an increase in hypomanic activity.

During the first year of Tom's life, he had been cared for largely by the maternal grandmother because his mother had to work. When he was two, his mother married and moved away from the grandmother, who had been the central figure in Tom's life. This loss was only one of many he had to endure. A year after the accident he was admitted to the hospital's research ward for several months, where his hypomanic behavior continued.

When he returned home, his feelings began to fluctuate widely. Times of family tranquillity were accompanied by a marked decrease of the hypomanic picture. However, a new stepfather, with whom he had good relations, was jailed for armed robbery, and a year later his mother was hospitalized for an acute depressive episode. Following each of these losses the boy had a long period of hypomania.

As Tom entered adolescence, episodes of hypomania began to alternate with periods of chronic depression. The depressive periods were set off by realistic concerns that he was not being accepted by his peers and by worries that girls would not find him attractive. But the hypomanic picture predominated. Tom's hypomania is unusual in one respect: it was precipitated by a severe injury. More often, this rare disorder breaks out for unknown reasons during a long bout of depressive illness.

We treated a girl, Dora, whose development was normal until she was eleven. Then, without apparent reason, she suddenly became aggressive and overtalkative, and boasted of sexual exploits. After several months of this behavior, which verged on mania, she became severely depressed, could not sleep, could not separate from her mother even briefly, and attempted to drown herself.

She switched into mania again, becoming endlessly talkative, engaging in dozens of activities, and in general acting as though in a state of euphoria or as if she were supremely pleased with herself and the world. Her later course and treatment are outlined in Chapter Six.

Another girl developed a childhood depression when she was between fifteen and twenty months old. At the age of four she had an episode of mania. She was hyperactive and irritable, couldn't sleep, her words tumbled out unintelligibly, and she had delusions that she was an airplane—and on two occasions "crash landed" into the wall.[9]

The basic differences between adults and children in the manic and hypomanic states are more a matter of degree than kind. Both groups share the tendency toward grandiosity, anger, and forced joviality; however, in children these phenomena usually have less intensity. Children are also less likely to act out these grandiose fantasies and irrational anger. The biggest difference lies in the fact that psychotic or delusional mania is extremely rare in children, while it is relatively common in manic adults.

The Best Source of Information: The Child

In diagnosing depression in children, many authorities contend that therapists should work on the basis of information derived not only from the child but from parents, teachers, and other important figures in the child's life. Our own experience, which is not unique, indicates that there is often a disparity between the material gathered from the child and that reported by other people. This disparity seems almost unique to depressive disorders in children; it is seldom seen in other conditions. Information from sources other than the child can be important, but the child seems to us to be the most reliable informant. In our experience, psychological testing in children—tests of their intelligence, aptitudes or attitudes—usually does not contribute significantly to accurate diagnosis of a depressive illness.

Various diagnostic questionnaires have been developed to help elicit complete information about the child's depressive symptoms, as well as other aspects of the child's behavior, thinking, and mood. The most widely used questionnaires are CAS (Children's Assessment Scale),[10] Dica (Diagnostic Inventory for Children and Adolescents),[11] ISC (Interview Schedule for Children),[12] and Kiddie-SADS (Child Version, Schedule of Affective Disorders and Schizophrenia).[13] There are complementary parent versions which add to the information that goes into making a final diagnosis. The above mentioned questionnaires are quite useful, especially in research settings.

THREE

The Development of Affective Disorders in Infants and Toddlers

Comprehensive studies[1-3] have now confirmed the high prevalence of anxiety and depressive disorders in the general adult population. Furthermore, most of the these adult disorders follow a chronic and intermittent course, despite improved psychotherapeutic and psychopharmacological efforts. These medical conditions cause not only untold emotional suffering to the patients and their families, but also great financial loss to the families and society in general. These facts have stimulated interest in primary prevention, as a fruitful approach to diminishing the prevalence of these disorders.

This approach has led to the investigation of ever younger children who might have either full-blown mood disorders or identifiable precursors. Several factors have encouraged such investigations. First, we have discovered that many adults with depressive or anxiety disorders can date the early signs or the full clinical picture of their illness to prepubertal and in some cases preschool years. Second, the children of parents with depressive and anxiety disorders have been found to have a significantly higher incidence of such disorders than the general population.[1] Conversely, in studying young children with depressive or anxiety disorders, one often finds the presence of the same or similar disorders in their parents and other first-degree relatives.

Depression in young children most commonly presents as a

dysthymic disorder, but can also appear as a major depressive disorder. Only rarely do we see bipolar disordered young children. In the same way, anxiety in young children most commonly presents as school phobias or other variants of separation anxiety, agoraphobia, avoidant disorder, and overanxious disorder. In studying and treating affectively disturbed young children, investigators have found that their parents report significant signs or symptoms of such disorders dating back to toddlerhood and even infancy. Such findings were among several developments that have led to the now burgeoning field of infant and toddler psychiatry, which in turn has given rise to the field of developmental psychopathology. This discipline concerns itself with integrating the vast body of knowledge about the interaction of human development with the natural course of mental illness. This new approach provides the theoretical framework for this chapter on affective disorders.

Let's clarify our use of the term *affective disorder*. This term is often used as a synonym for depression or mood disorders. In this chapter, however, the term "affective" will be used to cover anxiety as well as depressive phenomena, both of which involve disorders of affect. This approach seems justified, because in infants, anxious and depressive affects often cannot be differentiated. Also, as will be discussed later, there is a strong linkage (comorbidity) of anxiety and depressive disorders in childhood.

Developmental Issues

Affective Development

Many of the factors which determine future emotional development are already present at birth. According to the differentiation hypothesis of emotional expression,[4] there are only two basic emotions present at birth—undifferentiated distress and excitement. All the remaining emotions gradually evolve from these two, based on the maturation of the central nervous system and life experiences. In contrast, the discrete-emotions view[5] holds that the neural substrate for all emotions is already present at birth, and many of their characteristics (primarily facial espressions) can be elicited and observed even in early infancy.

Proponents of both theories agree that with the passage of time emotions become more differentiated and more complex, as they become connected to cognitive growth and language development and become increasingly internalized. Already in the first seven to nine months of life, observable emotions include anger, sadness, interest, fear, joy, and surprise. Obviously, the whole gamut of affects is crucial to both normal and abnormal personality development and functioning. We choose, however, to focus our attention on fear and sadness, which are the basis of affective disorders.

These same potentially pathological emotions serve crucial adaptive functions and are indispensable to the personality development of the infant and toddler—even to their very survival. The same fear that underlies all anxiety disorders in later life has a crucial survival role in signaling to the mother (or caregiver) that her child is in danger. In the same way, sadness, which underlies all depressive disorders in later life, elicits a positive emotional response in the form of nurturing, which may be crucial in maintaining an empathic bond between parent and child.

In the second year, cognitive growth promotes the first appearance of the additional emotions of guilt, shame, contempt and shyness. These emotions, too, have adaptive functions; further, they are crucial to moral development and vital to the survival of society. In early infancy these emotional states largely serve as signaling functions[6] and their expression is dependent on external events. They become, however, gradually internalized by the growing child, largely because of cognitive growth that enables the process of self-object differentiation.

During this gradual process of elaboration and internalization of affects, there are several milestones heralding specific stages of development. Somewhere around the eighth month of life, both separation anxiety and fear of strangers appear in most infants. These phenomena represent expectable developmental processes, which grow out of the child's ability to differentiate between himself, his parents, and other people. As a rule, these processes may last until the third or even the fourth year of life, proceeding alongside infant socialization.

While childhood depression has been generally recognized as a separate disorder for only about twenty-five to thirty years, development of depressive states in infants and young toddlers has been studied in great detail by several child psychoanalysts over the past century.

Object Relations

According to object relations theorists, there is little differentiation between the mother and the child in the first three months, even though it is recognized that the infant can recognize his mother already in the first week of life.[7] In the following months the infant becomes increasingly aware of distinct differences between himself and his mother.[8] This process of differentiation culminates at about eight months of age, when the phenomena of separation and stranger anxiety appear. In the ensuing months, the baby continues to move away from mother visually and literally in an effort to learn about the world around it, while still maintaining a strong tie to mother, who continues to function as a safe harbor.[9] In addition to attaining their own identity, infants begin to view the mother as a whole person, who contains both "good" nurturing qualities as well as "bad" punitive qualities. A process called object constancy[10] is attained at about one year of age.

During the second year of life the phase of so-called *separation-individuation* continues, with the infant making increasingly bold forays to explore the environment while returning periodically to the safety of the mother. If the mother rebuffs the child's periodic returns to her (rapprochement), mistaking it for a sign of excessive dependency, the child may feel rejected; such rejection, if repeated, may sow the seeds of a future depressive predisposition.[11]

Margaret Mahler and her associates described two sisters,

Ann and Susan, as good examples of the mother's special importance during the period when the child is becoming an individual. Toward the end of the first year of life, when children are
beginning to realize that there is more to the world than themselves and their mothers, Ann often sat at her mother's feet and
patiently begged for attention. Most often she begged in vain.
The investigators say that, as a result, she had little psychic energy for the next period of her development, the *practicing
phase*. During this period, Mahler found, the normal child takes
delight in trying out her new skills, particularly her ability to get
around by herself. She crawls or walks further and further from
her mother's feet and often becomes so absorbed in activities
that for long periods of time she seems oblivious to the mother's
presence. But Ann would make only brief excursions away from
her mother. This period, in which the usual child is exuberant,
lasted only a relatively short while for her, and she acted sub-
dued during most of it.

Later, Ann was plainly an unhappy little girl who could not
easily endure separation from her mother, did not get along well
with other adults and children, and showed little joy when her
mother returned after short, everyday absences. In one camera-
recorded scene she has a tantrum when her mother starts to
leave the room. At first she insists on going along but then gives
up and just stands there. Finally, when she retires to the play
area for the youngest babies, she turns her back on the others
and is clearly hurt and angry.

Ann is described as already vulnerable, already in trouble.
Unless through further experience the girl is amply compen-
sated for the rejections and other disappointments of her earliest
years, Mahler and her colleagues believe she may well develop
emotional problems.

By the time Ann's younger sister, Susan, entered the study,
the mother was still somewhat aloof and self-centered, but she
had mellowed. Every so often she would put the baby down and
bury herself in the newspaper. But Susan was by nature more
outward-going and determined than Ann. When she wanted her
mother's attention, she knew how to go about getting it. In one

photographed scene, she tugs at her mother's dress, looks beseechingly at her, and finally starts to pull herself up to her mother's knee. The viewer can almost hear the mother say, "Oh, the heck with it," as she puts the paper down and lovingly picks up the baby. Some time later, Susan looks distressed when her mother leaves the room, but—unlike Ann—soon turns happily to playing with others in the room. She is joyful when her mother returns. Mahler emphasizes that a child who has a good relationship with her mother shows relatively little tendency toward depression in early life and is better prepared emotionally than other children to handle what life offers.

Most people, while accepting the general concept of maternal rejection as one causative factor in the etiology of later depressive states, do not accept such a rigid timetable for this or any other single stage of emotional development because of the plasticity and adaptability of the human psyche.

The foregoing issues of separation and individuation are also tied to the beginning development of shame and guilt, well established in third year of life, which play a crucial role in depression.[12] Shame is tied to the development of self-esteem and requires reasonably completed individuation, while guilt is more dependent on the strength of the mother-child bond. Both shame and guilt are crucial to the development of depressive feelings. It may be for that reason that the first reported cases of childhood depression were detected in children nearing the end of the third year of life.

Another pioneer in this field was a psychiatrist named René Spitz. He had been interested in child development when in the 1940s he came upon 123 young children being raised in a South American nursery. He found that a number of them tended to withdraw from social contact, lose weight, have trouble sleeping, and become ill—behavior much like that being noticed by doctors nowadays in many older children who have suffered a loss and become depressed. Spitz called this behavior *anaclitic* (leaning upon) *depression*.[13] It lasted up to three months, after which some patients assumed a rigid, frozen posture.

Spitz searched for a common cause of such behavior. He

found that all the children who developed the symptoms cited above had been separated from their mothers somewhere between the sixth and eighth month of life for an unbroken period of at least three months. They had had no mother or good mother-substitute to lean upon, hence the term "anaclitic." When the separation ended in less than six months, Spitz found, usually the children suddenly turned "friendly, gay, approachable, and the withdrawal, disinterest, and rejection of the outside world, the sadness disappeared as if by magic."

How about the children whose mothers did not come back and who lacked a good substitute? Spitz was able to study that question in a foundling home, where the lost mothers had not been restored. Here the picture of depression was as clear-cut as in the nursery but continued to a more advanced stage. In the worst cases, the children became either stuporous, agitated, or retarded. It appeared that most could not be brought back to normal. In fact, twenty-four of the ninety-one who were studied died as a result of their condition, after reaching a stage of physical deterioration called marasmus.

Attachment

More than any other person, psychoanalyst John Bowlby[14] laid the groundwork for the theory of attachment. According to this theory, during the first year of life the child forms a strong bond to its mother through a series of predictable developmental stages, such as recognition of mother, smiling, separation anxiety, and fear of strangers. Normally this mother-child bond is firmly established by one year of age. Where Bowlby differs from the traditional analytic view is in his belief that the child is born with a set of innate mechanisms designed to evoke the maternal tie to the child. Prominent among these are smiling, crying, sucking, clinging, and following.

Bowlby and his collaborators noticed that children separated from their mothers, such as when hospitalized, went through a predictable sequence of emotional states. They named these protest, despair, and detachment. During the phase of protest, the baby is restless, angry, and vocal. Several days later, when the period of despair appears, the child becomes withdrawn, visibly sad, often refusing food and any contact with substitute caretakers. Finally, the period of detachment is characterized by more normal behavior, which includes a positive response to the caretaker. However, when, during this period, the mother returns, the child appears indifferent to her presence, indicating a still existing disturbance of the mother-child bond.

One of Bowlby's collaborators, Mary Ainsworth,[15] provided the first reliable method to (a) assess the attachment behavior, (b) classify the quality of such attachment, and (c) describe deviant forms of attachment. The method she devised is called the "Strange Situation." This involves a series of graded separations between infant and mother. The child's behavior is assessed each time he is reunited with his mother. A coding system has been devised that includes three major groups: Group A infants, labeled *avoidant,* are characterized by resisting contact with the mother upon reunion; Group B infants, labeled *securely attached,* approach the mother looking for proximity and contact; Group C infants, called *ambivalently attached,* are characterized by passivity, minimal exploration, and ambivalent reunion behavior with mother, marked by clinging or pushing the mother away. Each of these groups is divided into several subgroups representing variants of the above mentioned behaviors. Attachment behavior has been linked to the earliest forms of both anxiety and depression.

Shaeffer and Callender[16] also continued Bowlby's studies. They found that if infants *under* six months were separated from their mother by hospitalization, the previously mentioned three stages of disturbance did not occur. However, when the hospitalization occurred after six months or the appearance of separation anxiety and stranger anxiety, the stages of protest, despair, and detachment would invariably occur. This study indicates that the attachment bond between infant and mother must be well-established before its interruption causes psychic distress in the child.

Temperament

Current interest in the study of temperament dates from the beginning of the New York Longitudinal Studies of Alexander Thomas, Stella Chess and their coworkers in the mid 1950s.[17] They defined temperament as "the behavioral style of the individual child," incorporating the child's "characteristic tempo, rhythmicity, adaptability, energy expenditure, mood and focus of attention."[18] They established the following categories of temperament by using a content analysis of structured parent and teacher interviews: activity level, rhythmicity, approach or withdrawal after being exposed to a new stimulus, adaptability, threshold of responsiveness, intensity of reaction, quality of mood, distractibility, attention span and persistence.

These investigators defined three basic temperamental clusters: (1) "Easy children" are characterized by regularity, positive approach responses to new stimuli, high adaptability to change and mild or moderate intensity of mood that is predominantly positive. (2) "Difficult children" are characterized by irregularity in biological functions, negativity, withdrawal responses to new stimuli, slow adaptability to change, and intense, mostly negative mood responses. (3) The third group was termed the "slow-to-warm-up children." They are marked by a combination of negative responses of mild intensity to new stimuli with gradual adaptability after repeated contact. Their reactions are less intense. With repeated experiences and without pressure, such children gradually come to show quiet and positive interest and involvement.

Temperament is viewed by Chess and Thomas as in constant interaction with the environment. Within this interactional framework they introduced the concept of *goodness and poorness of fit*. At any age, if the individual's temperament, abilities, and motivations are consonant with the environmental expectations and demands, a goodness of fit will exist and one would expect good personality adjustment and functioning. If, however, the environmental demands and expectations are dissonant with the individual's temperament and abilities, poorness of fit will result, unfavorably influencing the individual's adjustment, functioning, and the course of psychological development.

Such an interactive approach implies that neither the child's temperamental and other characteristics nor the environmental demands are in themselves accurate predictors of future adaptation and functioning. Rather, the interaction between the growing child and its environment holds the key to future psychological development.[19] There are no formal data to support a strictly genetic or environmental etiology of temperament. Chess and Thomas followed 133 children from early infancy to adult life and found an impressive continuity over time of temperamental characteristics in many, but not all, of their subjects.

These investigators have reported that the children who belonged to the "difficult child" temperamental category were more likely to develop behavior disorders in early and middle childhood. They stressed, however, that behavioral disturbances can develop with any temperamental constellation, even that of the "easy child,"[19] if there exists a poorness of fit or dissonance between the child's capacities and the environmental demands and expectations.

Behavioral Inhibitions in Children:
A Possible Precursor to Anxiety Disorders

It is possible that precursors of anxiety disorders may manifest in infancy and toddlerhood as specific behaviors related to temperament. Children who are shy and inhibited withdraw; when confronted with a novel situation, "They typically stop their ongoing behavior, cease vocalizing, seek comfort from a familiar figure."[20] Some investigators associate these early temperamental traits with a risk for development of overanxious or avoidant disorder in childhood.[20] Jerome Kagan and his colleagues found that approximately 10 to 15 percent of children "appear predisposed to be irritable as infants, shy and fearful as toddlers and cautious and introverted when they reach school age." Their study also indicates that the tendency to approach or withdraw from a novel situation is a relatively enduring temperamental trait.[21,22]

A group at Harvard has ingeniously and extensively studied the role of this "behavioral inhibition to the unfamiliar" as a possible early precursor of anxiety disorders in childhood and adult anxiety disorders such as panic disorder and agoraphobia. To this end they studied children of parents with panic disorders and agoraphobia and those of parents with other psychiatric disorders.[23] The rates of behavioral inhibition in children of parents with panic disorder and agoraphobia were significantly higher than for the comparison group.

Next, the correlation between behavioral inhibition and childhood anxiety disorders was investigated in (1) the previously mentioned children of parents with panic disorders and agoraphobia and (2) an existing nonclinical sample of children followed by Kagan and associates identified at twenty-one months as either inhibited or uninhibited.[24] The investigators found that inhibited children had increased risk for multiple anxiety and phobic disorders, suggesting that behavioral inhibition may be associated with risk for anxiety disorders in children.

Studies of Infants and Toddlers of Bipolar (Manic-depressive) Parents

In our own research we began with what has become a landmark study. Seven male children with a bipolar parent were studied longitudinally, beginning at age one. Each boy was matched with a boy of the same age but with healthy parents.[25] In four of the index families the mother was bipolar; the father was bipolar in the remaining three families. All of the bipolar parents were on lithium and considered to be in remission at the time of the study.

The goal of the study was to evaluate attachment behavior, as well as the nature of affiliative expression and quality of social relationships, in the infants as they grew. A modified Ainsworth paradigm[26] was used at twelve, fifteen, eighteen months of age. The ratings of attachment were based on traditional measures developed by Ainsworth and her colleagues.[15] Ratings of emotional expression were measured by the methods developed by Harmon and Culp.[27]

Results of the study most relevant to a developmental perspective are: (1) over time, from twelve to eighteen months, insecure, ambivalent attachment increased in the infants with a bipolar parent; (2) these infants had less capacity for self-regulation of their emotional equilibrium, especially in handling fear and anger; and (3) only one of these infants showed at times a predominantly depressive mood.

Problem behaviors in the two groups of children were examined. Beginning when the boys were one year old, a staff member visited the home each month. Based on their cumulative observations and mothers' reports, the home visitors identified various psychological symptoms in the child. These included: phobias, sleep disturbances, eating problems, excessive shyness, passivity, hyperactivity, poor impulse control, self-punitive behaviors (for example, head banging), excessive dependency, social language problems, disturbances in regulation of affect, temper tantrums, echolalia, and resistance to physical contact. Children with a bipolar parent were rated as having both significantly more problems and more severe problems than children from control families.

Peer interactions were investigated at age two and a half years. At this time the control group was enlarged to twelve children. Each boy in the study group came to the laboratory for two sessions with his mother and a same-age playmate and his mother.[28] Children from bipolar families showed more inappropriate aggression, hurting their friends with greater frequency than controls did. They also showed substantially less altruism toward their peers, most noticeably reflected in less sharing.

The same children were used to investigate the development of object relations. Children from bipolar and normal families performed similarly on tests of object permanence and self-recognition. However, children from bipolar families were more frequently judged insecure in their attachment relationship to the mother at age twenty-six months (86 percent in bipolar families vs. 30 percent in controls). Early impairments in object relations were manifested in tasks that involved interactions with people.

The same seven sons of bipolar parents and their controls were given a psychiatric evaluation at age six.[29] On the basis of these assessments diagnoses were made using *DSM-III* criteria. In the group with bipolar parents, three had a unipolar depressive disorder, three had a conduct disorder, three had an overanxious disorder, and three had a separation anxiety disorder. All seven children had at least one *DSM-III* diagnosis, and the majority had two or more diagnoses. Of the twelve control children, three had separation anxiety disorder and two had simple phobia; none had depressive or conduct disorder diagnoses.

The authors also participated in a study of toddlers of one hundred and twenty families in which mothers either had no history of psychiatric illness or suffered from a major or minor affective disorders. All parents were given a psychiatric interview and were diagnosed according to the Research Diagnostic Criteria of Robert Spitzer and his colleagues.[30] The children ranged in age from fifteen months to fifty-four months and the sexes were evenly distributed.

To be considered at high risk for the later development of psychopathology, a child must have been rated as dysfunctional in each of these four areas: (1) the quality of the child's relationship with his mother; (2) the child's dominant mood; (3) the child's ability to regulate his mood; and (4) the child's mastery in play both when observed with mother and when observed with the psychiatrist. Of the one hundred and twenty children, sixteen were considered dysfunctional in both settings. These sixteen children were considered to be the most disturbed in the entire sample[31] and presented four patterns or syndromes of maladaptation, as described below.

Syndrome 1 (Socially and Emotionally Isolated): There was only one child in this group and he displayed a detached style of relating to mother. In most scenes he initiated almost no interaction with his mother and often ignored her presence. There seemed to be little warmth, empathy, or caring between them. The child's style of mood regulation was overcontrolled. His affect was blunted even when he appeared annoyed with his mother. With the psychiatrist he never lost control of his moods; rather, for thirty minutes he was entirely mute. His pattern of mastery in play was characterized by minimal play activity. He functioned best when playing on his own in the presence of mother. This was the child who worried us most. His lack of emotional expression and of social relatedness suggested a schizoid quality to his evolving personality. Neither parent of this child had a psychiatric diagnosis.

Syndrome 2 (Dysphoric): Three girls displayed this pattern. They related to their mother in an emotionally isolated yet physically close style. These children initiated very little interaction with their mother, and their dominant mood was one of sadness or apathy. Often they were simply very still, doing and saying little. They were easily frustrated and revealed few resources for coping, often becoming whiny or clingy. One of the girls began head banging when mother lay down for a nap. None of these children could be separated from her mother for the psychiatric interview. Since each of the girls cried bitterly, her mother had to be allowed to stay for the entire interview. All displayed anhedonia (lack of pleasure in activities that would be expected to be pleasurable), showing little interest in play materials, almost no exploration in the laboratory apartment, withdrawal from the psychiatrist and from the novel play materials he presented.

These children appeared clinically depressed. Each of them had a mother with a unipolar major depressive disorder. In addition, one of the fathers had a recurrent major depression and one was absent from the home; one father had no psychiatric diagnosis.

Syndrome 3 (Angry and Anxious): This pattern was observed in eight cases (four boys, four girls). Their dominant mood was anger, alternating with anxiety. These children demonstrated little ability to regulate their moods, often expressing their anger by throwing temper tantrums, acting aggressively toward their mothers, and smashing toys. During the psychiatric interview, many of these children appeared very fearful and lost control completely, weeping excessively and clinging to mother.

The anxious and angry children showed two patterns of poor coping with play materials. One group showed some curiosity and appropriate play with toys; however, when they were faced with frustration or adult limit-setting, their play became dysfunctional. They fell apart and often became aggressive toward either the toy or the adult. The other play pattern was seen in children who appeared so angry that they were out of control. These children showed minimal interest in play materials and spent most of their time in disorganized activity, temper tantrums, or aimless wandering.

Two of the mothers in this group had major depression and two had minor depression, while four had no psychiatric diagnosis. Among the fathers, four had major depression, three had no psychiatric diagnosis, and one was absent.

Syndrome 4 (Structure Dependent): This group consisted of four boys. These children showed the best relationship to their mothers of all the high-risk children, and at times were able to behave warmly and empathically. They also showed a wide range of emotions, including pleasure and joy. However, when mother withdrew her attention, these boys had difficulty maintaining control; they often became angry, uncooperative, and verbally or physically aggressive toward the mother. Without structure, they became oppositional, belligerent, and excessively angry. Play was good when supervised. With toys enabling aggression, there were problems with impulse control, and without adult attention these children became angry and even destructive of play materials.

At times they were able to show joy and pleasure and to play competently with adult supervision. However, they appeared to have little if any ability to maintain self-control without an adult structuring the situation. All mothers in this group had a mood disorder: one had major depression, one was bipolar, and two had minor depression. Among the fathers, two had major depression, one was alcoholic, and one had no psychiatric diagnosis.

Radke-Yarrow and her colleagues studied these same families using a different methodology.[32] These changes were made: (1) in addition to the psychiatric interviews of the children, the maternal report on the Child Behavior Checklist (CBC) was used; (2) while our study focused on the most disturbed children, Radke-Yarrow chose to cast a much wider net, including much less disturbed children.

The psychiatric assessment of the same toddlers reported on above yielded the following results. Fifty-four percent of children of unipolar mothers, 43 percent of children of normal mothers, and only 18 percent of children of bipolar mothers had a "problem status," which included such areas of concern as separation anxiety, generalized anxiety, disruptive behavior, and depressive symptoms. When the psychiatric assessment of the children was combined with the mothers' reports, the following results were obtained: 66 percent of the children of unipolar mothers, 46 percent of those of normal mothers, and only 25 percent of those of bipolar mothers had a "problem status."

Three of the five components of this "problem status" are of special interest. Depressive symptoms were found in 7 percent of the toddlers of unipolar mothers and none in the children of either normal or bipolar mothers. Symptoms of anxiety were present in 34 percent of the toddlers with unipolar mothers, 30 percent of those with normal mothers, and only 9 percent of those with bipolar mothers. The "disruptive-aggressive" symptoms cluster was found in 34 percent of toddlers with unipolar mothers but in only 14 percent of these with both normal and bipolar mothers.

The results of our and Radke-Yarrow's approaches to this study of one hundred and twenty toddlers differ somewhat, probably due to a different methodology; however, they agree on two fundamental issues: (1) serious depressive disorder is very rare in toddlers and occurs predominantly in the offspring of unipolar parents, (2) the frequency of serious psychopathology in toddlers of bipolar parents does not differ from that in children of normal controls.

In the initially described family study,[25] the infants and toddlers of bipolar parents showed serious disturbances from at least the second year of life. In contrast, the toddlers of bipolar parents in the second family study did not differ from normal controls in the rate of psychopathology. This disparity may be related to the fact that the bipolar parents in the first study were severely ill, had all been on medication, and had experienced one or more psychiatric hospitalizations. The children's home environment was extremely disturbed and marked by disorganization, conflict, chaos, unpredictability, and alienation. The bipolar parents in the second study, on the other hand, had much less severe illness. None had been hospitalized, few were on medication, and their family life was not marked by the extremes noted in the first study.

These studies demonstrate that the risk of psychopathology in offspring of mood-disordered parents parallels the severity of parental psychopathology.

Clinical Issues

Anxiety disorders of early childhood grow out of two normal developmental milestones characterized by anxiety, namely, separation anxiety and stranger anxiety. Behavioral inhibition occurring in infancy is often a precursor of future anxiety disorder. Anxiety disorders in infancy and toddlerhood are worrisome if they present in an exaggerated form, but would rarely be diagnosed as pathological before the age of three.

In contrast, most clinicians, with some notable exceptions (including Margaret Mahler), don't view depression as a part of normal psychological development in infants and toddlers. However, we do recognize depressive-like states in this age group, which are environmentally caused and labeled by *DSM-IV* as "reactive attachment disorder of infancy or childhood."

This condition was called "anaclitic depression" by Spitz,[13] "hospitalism" by Bakwin,[33] and despair by Bowlby.[14]

Reactive attachment disorder is characterized by persistent failure to initiate or respond to most social interactions. These infants exhibit a lack of visual tracking, reciprocal play, and vocal imitation or playfulness; they are apathetic and show little or no spontaneity. At a later age one sees lack of curiosity or social interest. This condition is always brought on by grossly pathogenic care, as evidenced by one of the following: (1) persistent disregard of the child's basic emotional needs for comfort, stimulation, and affection; (2) persistent disregard for the child's basic physical needs, including nutrition, housing, and protection from outside danger; (3) repeated changes of primary caregiver so that stable attachments are not possible.

Depressive states are not seen as normal developmental stages in infancy, as are separation anxiety and fear of strangers, which have a strong survival value for navigation in a hostile world. Nevertheless, Bowlby[14] and Engel[34] have argued that depressive mood states in infants and toddlers also have survival value, in that they evoke sympathy and primary care-taking, and lead to the child's being reunited with his mother or provided adequate substitute mothering and improved care.

FOUR

"I Wish I Wasn't Alive"

Children under fourteen rarely commit suicide. Recently, however, suicide in this age group seems to be on the rise. The age-specific suicide rate for children under fourteen was 0.5 per 100,000 in 1991.[1] According to the latest report of the Centers for Disease Control and Prevention, children aged ten to fourteen are committing suicide twice as often as in 1980 and are increasingly using guns to kill themselves.[2]

For some children, divorce, the formation of a new family with stepparents and stepsiblings, or moving to a new community and/or new school can be very unsettling and can intensify self-doubts. In some cases, suicide appears to be a "solution." Depression and suicidal feelings are treatable mental disorders. The child or adolescent needs to have his or her illness recognized and appropriately diagnosed.

A high rate of nonfatal suicidal behavior among children six to twelve has been reported.[3] It is disturbing to hear these stories.

An eight-year-old girl sat in her room carefully writing her last will and testament. Whatever she had, she wrote, was to go to her sister, mother, and father. She added that she loved them all. Then she picked up a rock that was almost too heavy for her to handle, carried it downstairs to where her father sat reading a book, knelt in from of him, and said, "Daddy, would you crush my head, please?" When her father, whom she loved very much, would not indulge her in this one carefully thought-out wish, she was crestfallen. Sobbing, she ran from the house.

The father, of course, was greatly disturbed. He called to his wife, and they rushed up to the girl's room and found a suicide note. Almost frantic, they began telephoning around and eventually reached us. We saw the family the next day and diagnosed the child as having a bipolar disorder.

Another girl, about eleven, tried to drown herself. She walked out into the ocean until she was almost up to her neck. Then she plunged forward and let herself sink. But the waves pushed her back toward the land, and soon she was on the beach again. She tried again and again, fortunately with the same result.

A boy of about the same age tried walking in front of moving automobiles. But they all stopped in time or else managed to avoid him by swerving.

Then there was a boy, seven years old, who was seriously depressed. He thought he could kill himself with a pitchfork and reasoned that he could prop up the fork in a corner of the barn—prop it up very carefully so that a light disturbance, a footfall even, would send it falling. As soon as he had positioned it, he would run back a little way and then rush forward. His plan called for the fork to fall toward him, and as he rushed, its tines would pierce his stomach and he would die. But it didn't work out that way. Over and over he tried. Each time the fork fell harmlessly to the floor without touching him. Disappointed and despairing, he later related how he felt: "What a complete flop I am. I can't even kill myself!"

These illustrative cases are reminders that suicide attempts, in young childhood, are not infrequent.

Suicides as Accidents

Then, too, there is reason to believe that some children killed in accidents are actually victims of suicides. There was a boy in his early teens, for instance, who had been using LSD. A number of

LSD users had a theory that if you swallowed some of the drug and then pulled your necktie or scarf or a rope tightly around your neck, you would get an intense sexual feeling. But this boy went into the cellar with no clothes on, stepped onto a chair, made a noose in one end of a piece of rope, tied the other end to the rafters, put the noose around his neck, swallowed an LSD tablet, and then kicked the chair out from under himself. His father found him hanging there. He had been dead for some hours.

One of us saw the family. They made it very clear that the child had been distraught for a long time. They also made it clear how upset the whole family had been over various matters. They added that he was a bright youngster and had been doing well in school. There was never any question in our minds that the boy had intended to kill himself. Maybe he wanted to make it look as if he had been trying to get a sexual experience by swallowing LSD and tightening something about his neck. But he certainly had enough intelligence to know that when he kicked that chair out, there was no tomorrow. The family insisted, however, that this was an accidental death, and the coroner went along with them.

Such an event—a suicide going down in the record as an accidental death—is fairly common with adults. For example, there is reason to believe that many people killed in single-car accidents deliberately set out to take their life. Some adolescent patients have told us that when especially distraught they have aimed at tree trunks, hoping that after the crash they would never wake up. Or they've driven recklessly, hoping for an accident that once and for all would put an end to their intense depression.

Nathan Kline, a noted scholar on affective disorders and suicide, believes that the actual number of suicides each year is likely to be many times larger than official estimates. That's because most suicides are not reported as such—"for religious reasons, for insurance purposes, and most often because of uncertainty, as in automobile accident. . . ." Also, Kline believes, for every suicide there may be at least ten attempts. Kline writes:[4]

The depressive is often quite consciously guilty, and what he feels guilty about is being depressed. He has failed in his own eyes the test of will and spirit. He blames himself for his weakness, and he assumes that others blame him, too. Indeed, he often is blamed by those around him. Thus, we believe it is the overwhelming guilt that impels some depressives to commit suicide. They are driven to do something about their condition, they cannot master it, and so in one final act of resolution they end the dismal struggle.

From Toddlers to College Students

Among college students, where the normal pressures of late adolescence are joined by such added burdens as worry about taking the right course or joining the right social group, struggles to do well in academic courses or extracurricular activities, the money squeeze, and the competition of fellow students, suicide ranks second only to accidents as the leading cause of death.

Very young children, too, sometimes make suicidal attempts or gestures. For example, four-year-old David wrapped himself in a blanket and set a match to it. Just as the corner of the blanket caught fire, his foster mother discovered him. Later, in a psychiatric interview, the boy said he was sad because he missed his mother. He repeatedly climbed atop pieces of tall furniture and threw himself into the air, only to be caught by the therapist. Asked why he was trying to hurt himself, he replied: "Because David is a bad boy. There will be no more David." Later the therapist asked, "David, why did you try to burn yourself?" He answered, "Because I am not a good boy. David has to die." Therapist: "Why?" David: "Because my mommy wants me to."

Another boy, Jeffrey, three, was referred to a psychiatrist because for a month he had been repeatedly throwing himself down a fifteen-step flight of stairs, sustaining many bruises. He had also been banging his head on the floor, causing bleeding. His explanation: "Jeff is bad, and bad boys have to die." During a psychiatric interview it developed that there was a new baby in the house, and "My mommy doesn't like me but likes my brother." Jeff threw a boy doll from the top of a toy truck and said, "Boy has to die."

Then there was young Benji. He had temper tantrums, destroyed furniture, and bit and pinched his foster mother. During treatment he almost stopped eating for two weeks. He bit himself till he bled, and threatened to jump in front of cars. In therapy he made a boy doll fall from he dollhouse stairs and from the top of play blocks. When the therapist asked why the little boy was hurting himself, Benji said, "He is a bad boy. Nobody loves him." Therapist: "Why?" Benji: "Because Benji was bad. Now he has to get hurt."

Benji made it clear through his play that he was afraid of losing his foster mother, that he did not want to go to his biological mother, and that he wanted to die.

All three of these toddlers had suffered losses—a parent leaving or a new sibling arriving—and were craving mother's attention. They responded with a equation often seen in the young children we have studied: Sad = Mad = Bad. Their self-destructive behavior served all three elements. They attempted to relieve their loss and sadness through attention-seeking. They tried to handle their anger, rage, and frustration through acting out. At the same time they tried to pay for their badness, their sins, through self-harm.

Another toddler, wanting to commit suicide because he considered himself bad, took many aspirin tablets. A girl of the same age assaulted animals, other children, and her mother, and took a number of her mother's antidepressant pills.

One major study of factors in a child's life that seem related to suicidal behavior was conducted by Cynthia R. Pfeffer and coworkers at Cornell University Medical School.[5,6] The investigators constructed eight "Child Suicidal Potential Scales," each intended to detect and measure a number of circumstances that might be related to such a behavior—actions that might lead to death or serious injury, or thoughts that might do the same if acted upon.

Fifty-eight children aged six to twelve were studied. All had undergone stress of various kinds—most commonly, worry about school failure, disturbed friendships, fears of parental punishment, or changes in the family or at school. Considerably more than half of the children—forty-two out of a total of fifty-eight—were found to have suicidal ideas, to have threatened suicide, or to have tried to commit suicide.

Certain feelings or attitudes distinguished the suicidal from the nonsuicidal children. These were: depression, hopelessness, worthlessness, and the wish to die. Also, the suicidal children were significantly more preoccupied with thoughts of death, more worried about members of their family dying, and more upset by the actual death of someone close to them. During the six months before the study began, the suicidal children were reported to have become increasingly depressed and hopeless. The mothers of the suicidal children were more frequently depressed than the mothers of nonsuicidal children. The belief that death is a pleasant state was related significantly to the degree of seriousness of the suicidal children's behavior. Also, significantly more of the suicidal children worried about doing poorly in school.

In short, this study offers strong evidence that suicidal thoughts or behavior are common symptoms among severely disturbed children from six to twelve years old. Many of the factors found to be related to suicidal thoughts or behavior in this age group are similar to those commonly recognized in adults and adolescents. The investigators maintain that a routine part of the psychiatric evaluation of children should be the assessment of the risk of such behavior.

Pfeffer[7] did a six-to-eight-year follow-up of one hundred and thirty-three patients similar to the ones described in the study above. Forty percent of these children had reported suicidal ideas when they were first hospitalized, while 36 percent reported suicide attempts (a self-inflicted act with the intent to cause death).

At the time of follow-up, six to eight years later, 15 percent of the patients had attempted suicide and half of the attempters reported multiple suicide attempts. Among all these children, whether at first hospitalization or during the follow-up years, only one factor could be found that separated the suicidal children from the nonsuicidal: the presence of a mood disorder.

The initial studies of childhood suicidal behavior were inpatient studies, that is, studies of hospitalized children. In recent years Maria Kovacs has begun to report on her work with outpatients. One study reports on sixty sequentially referred outpatients ages eight to thirteen.[8] When first seen, 66 percent of these children had admitted suicidal ideas while 9 percent had made suicide attempts. All the children in the study were suffering from mood disorders. There were no differences in rates of suicidal thoughts or attempts between boys and girls.

These patients were followed for up to twelve years. The results of the follow-up indicate that for these children the rate of suicidal ideation was remarkably stable, while the rate of suicide attempts climbed steadily from late latency until mid-adolescence (eight to seventeen years). During these follow-up years, the children who had suicidal thoughts or made suicidal attempts continued for the most part to have some form of mood disorder. As the children entered adolescence, a clear sex difference began to appear. A larger proportion of girls than boys had suicidal ideas and made suicidal attempts. For all these children, when conduct disorders and substance abuse disorders were superimposed on an underlying mood disorder, a higher risk for suicidal behavior was noted.

Suicidal and Aggressive Behavior

Pfeffer has expanded the research reported above by studying the relationship between suicidal and assaultive behavior in children.[9] Her subjects were approximately one hundred children admitted to a hospital psychiatric ward. About one-fourth were diagnosed as depressed. The subjects were divided into four categories: nonassaultive nonsuicidal; suicidal-only; assaultive-only; and assaultive suicidal. Among the suicidal-only children, the most common diagnosis was depression. The greatest contrast was noted between the suicidal-only and assaultive-only children. Children in the first group were relatively well adjusted and were beset, in the main, by grief over the suicide of a loved person or by other extreme environmental pressures, such as loss of a parent or a major move. On the other hand, the assaultive-only children were marked by constitutional or temperamental difficulties such as chronic anger and assaultive tendencies, by lying, stealing, and truancy, and by bad experiences, such as those caused by parental violence.

Pfeffer speculates that suicidal behavior and assaultiveness are two independent patterns of behavior, produced by different factors. Other investigators, including ourselves, do not agree. The infant study described in Chapter Three, whose subjects are babies of manic-depressive parents, has yielded some striking findings about the relationship between depression and anger.[10] Many of the children showed feelings of anger toward their parents. These feelings were much more intense than those shown by children from homes where there is no depressive illness.

In a related study, David Shaffer, at Columbia University, found that suicidal behavior often correlates not only with depressive symptoms, but with antisocial or aggressive symptoms as well.[11] Unlike Pfeffer, he also concludes that inwardly and outwardly directed aggression can both occur in the same individual.

Moreover, Joachim Puig-Antich, also of Columbia University, has found that 40 percent of children with major depressive disorders also have conduct disorders.[12] If the depressive disorder is successfully treated, the conduct disorder improves as well.

The conflicting conclusions noted above result from honest differences of opinion, as well as from the fact that each research team worked with a different sample of children. There is more commonly an association between antisocial acting-out behavior and depressive phenomena, including suicide, in children from lower socioeconomic class, while those from middle or upper social class families are more likely to internalize angry feelings and relatively rarely show overtly aggressive behavior. Our own clinical experience indicates that aggressive behavior and depression may occur in the same person. Freud himself saw the aggressive component in depression, as opposed to simple mourning.[13] Such a tie between depression and aggression seems clearer in suicidal children than in most other depressed children.

There are several predisposing factors that make a child more vulnerable to attempted or completed suicide. Some of Pfeffer's more recent studies[14] indicate that normal school children commonly have ideas about suicide although they usually don't attempt suicide. However, under severe environmental stress, even normal children under twelve years of age can commit suicide, as was seen in the aftermath of Hurricane Andrew in South Florida. As reported in *Newsweek,* April 5, 1993:

Andrew's most disturbing recent aftermath:
A flurry of suicide attempts by some
of the storm's youngest survivors

> In the past three months, more than a dozen Dade elementary-school students have tried to kill themselves. School officials say that they include a 7-year-old who jumped from a second-floor balcony, another who tried to hang himself with an electrical cord, an 8-year-old who lay down in front of a school bus, and a boy of 10 who was hospitalized after swallowing fistfuls of aspirin and Nyquil. Most of the children are now seeing therapists. A psychologist quoted a number of the children saying, "I can't take it anymore."

These children, like other children who have been through severe environmental stress, are showing symptoms of post-traumatic stress disorder, delayed shock marked by recurrent nightmares, flashbacks, and depression.

Another contributing factor to suicide is childhood sexual abuse. One thirteen-year-old patient overdosed on pills when she had flashbacks of being raped by her grandfather. These reported flashbacks of abuse were met with disbelief by all her family and even her therapist. This may have led her to feel that there was "no way out," no help possible, so that suicide became the only option.

Summing Up

Completed suicide is relatively rare before adolescence, but it seems to be on the rise.

About half of the depressed children we have seen had suicidal thoughts. But only a few attempted suicide and were successful at it. Some children commit suicide but their deaths are listed as accidents—probably in large part because of family shame and because society shuns the idea that a child would take his own life. But young, bright toddlers have threatened suicide and even made attempts to carry out the threats.

Suicidal children have been found to be depressed, to have lost all hope, to feel worthless, and to have a wish to die. They think of death more often than other children and worry more about members of their family dying. The mothers of suicidal children are more often depressed than mothers of nonsuicidal children. Often a suicidal child will also tend to be aggressive or assaultive.

How to Spot Potential Suicides

Any suicidal talk and gestures should be taken very seriously, since they are usually a cry for help. Many of the symptoms of impending suicide are similar to those of depression. If one or more of these signs occur, teachers and parents need to talk to the child and, if the signs persist, get professional help:

- Change in eating and sleeping habits
- Withdrawal from friends, family, and social activities
- Violent actions, rebellious behavior, or running away
- Drug and alcohol use
- Unusual neglect of personal appearance
- Marked personality change
- Persistent boredom, difficulty concentrating, or a decline in the quality of schoolwork
- Loss of interest in pleasurable activities
- Intolerance for praise or rewards

Help is even more urgently needed if the child is preoccupied with death and suicide.

When a child says, "I want to kill myself," or "I'm going to commit suicide," parents and teachers should always take the statement seriously. If several of the signs listed above are present, it is a good idea to gently ask about feelings of depression or ideas about suicide. Such questions will reassure the child that somebody cares and give him an opportunity to ventilate his feelings. Children, like adults, almost always discuss their suicide with a friend, a family member, or a doctor within forty-eight hours of attempting suicide.

The Causes of
Childhood Depression

What sets off a depressive illness? Presumably stress. It is
known that adults who become depressed and are admitted
to a psychiatric clinic have undergone a greater number of
stressful events than people who have been admitted to a clinic
for treatment of nonpsychiatric illness. But what are sources of
stress in childhood?

Many Factors May Be at Work

Eight-year-old Dorothy was first seen by us because her mother
reported that the girl had made suicidal threats. She was described as always having been sad and withdrawn, and as having
much trouble separating from her mother in the normal course
of becoming independent. She cried a great deal. Her father had
left home when she was still a toddler but returned at infrequent
intervals. Eventually the mother began living with another man.
Both of these men had a good relationship with Dorothy's older
brother but were very abusive of the girl. In addition, abuse,
anger, and violence were common in the family environment.
The mother, who said she herself had been unwanted as a child,
had been intensely depressed most of her life.

This case history illustrates several of the factors that are
found so often in the background of depressed children—rejec-

tion and depreciation, a depressed parent, and early loss of a significant person. Dorothy, when still quite young, had lost a person who was naturally of decided significance in her life—her father. Also, her father and the man who took his place rejected the girl, as shown by their abusive treatment of her. Finally, her mother had been depressed most of her own life. This circumstance suggests several possibilities. By associating with her mother, Dorothy may have picked up her mother's behavior, particularly the way she reacted to unpleasant events in her life. Or, the mother may have passed on to Dorothy biological vulnerability that made both persons succumb to depression when circumstances triggered it. In addition, the mother's depression made her less available to meet the girl's need for nurture. Thus, both Dorothy's environment and inherited biological makeup may have been at work here.

Sometimes only one factor appears significant. For instance, a ten-year-old-girl, Betsy, was ostracized by the entire family because she was her mother's child by a previous marriage. Her inability to throw off or make light of this rejection led to a serious depression.

As these examples suggest, there are two main groups of causes of depression. In Betsy's case one of these—environmental—seems to have been important. In Dorothy's case, a biological factor and an environmental one may have been combined.

The Family and Other Social Causes

Ten-year-old Janine lives with her mother, 31, two full siblings, and three half-siblings. The parents are divorced. We first saw Janine, an attractive but very quiet child, because she was deeply depressed and had made suicidal threats. The staff at the school where she was in third grade described her as being withdrawn, having few friends, and learning only slowly.

Her mother, a tall, slim, pretty woman, appears to be a concerned, even doting, parent. When she talks about Janine, the mother becomes depressed, and it is hard to tell when she is speaking of her daughter and when she is referring to her own lonely, depressed childhood. Her daughter's problem arose, the mother believes, mainly because the father rejected Janine and favored his other children. She speculates also that her own negative, unhappy life has somehow rubbed off on her daughter.

When Janine was ten months old she was hospitalized and then operated on for a small tumor near the surface of the brain. After three months in the hospital she came home frightened of everything. She clung to her mother and slept with her for weeks. This was the period when the mother was especially depressed and when serious conflict broke out between husband and wife. When Janine was two, the parents separated and the mother began going to an outside job. The maternal grandmother took care of the children.

Janine remained a frightened child, insisting on sleeping with the lights on, until she was six. Now she sleeps in the same room as a younger sister and is like a mother to her. She spends much of her playtime at a neighborhood recreation center but has no close friends. She often complains of headaches and fatigue.

The mother says that she herself married to get away from home. She acts toward Janine and her other children much as if she were their sibling, telling them all of her problems. In front of them she tells other people that she dislikes males and hopes that her girls won't have any children so that they can escape the burdens that have been placed upon her. The mother feels hopeless about Janine's ability to lead a happy life, and feels the same way about herself. She does maintain a neat, quiet, orderly home.

We see the mother as a depressed, dependent woman whose children are all she feels she can cling to. When she says that Janine has a problem, she's right: the child has taken into herself her mother's problem. In the words of the late Anna Freud, "They followed the mother into her depression."[1] In addition, the mother's difficulties in coping with her own life made her less available at a very vulnerable time in her child's life. Janine also had to bear the brunt of an early hospitalization, as well as depreciation and rejection by the father. As in the previous case, the possibility exists that the mother has passed on to Janine a genetic predisposition for depression.

In the past a child like Janine might have been misdiagnosed. Her sad mood would have been disregarded and her depression overlooked. Very often in the past such children have been felt to be exceptionally well adjusted because they were quiet and would sit peacefully, making no trouble for anyone. So the misdiagnosis was actually appreciation of their depression and quietness. In other children, withdrawal would be seen not as an indication of sadness but as evidence of their antisocial attitude. As a result, they would be encouraged to socialize—to mingle with other children, to participate in games and sports, to speak out in groups. But when they are encouraged to make such an effort without their being offered help for their depression, it just makes them feel more uncomfortable than they are and worse about themselves than they already do.

The most disastrous form of misdiagnosis was to view the child as mildly retarded because his or her grades were quite poor—and the grades of depressed children are often quite poor, since they have difficulty focusing sufficient interest and attention on their schoolwork. The depressed child who was considered mildly retarded might carry the label "retarded" for the rest of his life.

We often see depressed children or families who like Janine's ensnare their members in an abnormally tight bond that fosters unusual closeness and dependency. This has been called enmeshment.[2] We are not talking about families commonly described as close-knit, whose members show a warm interest in one another and help one another when help is needed. They keep in touch with the other members through letters, telephone calls, birthday cards, and so on. They like to hold family reunions.

Sam's case is an example of a family with abnormally close bonds. Sam, who is ten years old, came to our attention after he had threatened to overdose on his mother's antidepressant medication. Sam's rather large family and various relatives all lived in the same dwelling and clung together. The boy had a fear of

leaving home even to play, and other family members rein-
forced this fear by portraying the outside world as dangerous.
His mother and an aunt were also frightened of leaving the
house, so they were unable to find jobs or to make friends.
Whenever Sam did go out, he would frequently telephone to see
how his mother was: he was afraid she would harm herself.

In other families, one or more members are excluded from
the family circle. Here, too, there is a boundary—only somebody
is fenced out rather than in. In such families we often have
found a striking lack of communication between the excluded
members and the rest of the family. In family therapy sessions,
the excluded member would sit apart from the rest of the family
and be ignored not only in casual conversation but in formal
therapy exchanges as well.

When the mother of one boy who had been hospitalized for a
depressive illness visited the hospital, she often sat alone in his
room watching television while he played in the hallway. When
he came back into his room, the mother made no effort to engage him in play or conversation. Visits were always short, and
mother and son would watch the same television program without exchanging a word. This boy's mother's lack of emotional
involvement contributed to his problem.

Another family pattern involves a situation in which the
child is accepted provided she or he measures up to very high
standards set by the family in one or more areas. Often these
children are expected to excel in order to boost the family's self-
esteem. Ten-year-old Frances, for example, learned to be a com-
petent swimmer by the time she was five. The parents became
increasingly involved in her aquatic activities and began to expect her to become a champion. But the girl really wasn't as tal-
ented as the family's wishes and expectations led them to believe. Each failure to win a competition was followed by the
family's open expression of disappointment—and, ultimately,
disapproval. The child began feeling guilty for having let the parents down and saw herself first as inadequate and then a failure.
This lowering of self-esteem was followed by a prolonged period
of depression.

Because family distress frequently is present in the background of depressed children, families should always be evaluated by the treating mental health professional. Direct and lengthy observations of the family are needed. Perhaps the school, the church, or the pediatrician could help families recognize warning signs. But, sadly, many children don't receive professional attention until they are already seriously depressed.

Childhood depression is very strongly correlated with depression in a parent. In most of our cases at least one parent showed clinical evidence of depression, and some had been treated for this condition. In others the depression was manifested as a subtle mood disorder that never reached a level requiring treatment.

Parental depression sometimes may be inherited by the child. Or it may affect the child because he or she has identified with the sick parent, or because the latter's illness has lessened parental involvement with the child, leaving him feeling alone or rejected. Some of our child patients improved rapidly as soon as they were separated from their parents—a phenomenon we often observed when a child was hospitalized. Apparently this dramatic improvement occurs when the child has not taken in, or internalized, the parent's depression; in other words, he has not made the parent's depression a part of himself. We have seen cases where the child's chronically depressed mood improved within one or two days of hospitalization and recurred only during parental visits. On the other hand, those children in whom the process of internalization seemed to be already operating remained depressed even while they were away from their parents. This was true of children as young as six years of age. One can also argue that children who remain depressed even when away from their depressed parent do so because their depression stems mainly from genetic factors.

Separations from Loved Persons or Places[3]

In many of our patients, frequent separations for several months or more from important people or places have taken place.

These separations are deemed particularly harmful if they occurred during the child's first few years. Episodes of reattachment to the original loved person were often followed by further separations. The substitute caretakers during the time of separation were frequently indifferent to the child or provided an unstable environment. This type of loss is most commonly associated with chronic depression.

Loss of a Strong Attachment

Some episodes of depression are precipitated by the sudden and usually permanent loss of a much loved person as a result of death, divorce, or a move away from the environment the child has gotten used to. The important factors seem to be an excessive dependency on the loved person or place before the loss and the absence of an appropriate substitute afterward.

Loss of involvement with a loved person may sometimes take a more subtle form. A central figure in the child's life suddenly withdraws his or her interest in the child while maintaining a close physical presence. The adult's loss of interest is usually related to such events as illness, personal tragedy, or new involvement with other people, as in the case of remarriage or a new baby in the home.

When there's a new baby, the older sibling often reacts in one of two ways. One that we see very often is the expression of general hostility. The older child will do everything to be bad, including messing up his or her room and thus creating trouble for father and mother, crying and carrying on when the parents go out, and acting like the new baby by regressing in toilet-training habits.

The second common reaction to a new baby may be called overcompensation: the older child becomes just the most loving person possible. Instead of showing hostility directly, the older child will be the nicest little person possible toward the family's newest member.

What can parents do? The best time to step in is long before the baby is born. You can talk to your children about the new baby that's coming. You can do everything possible to try to make them part of the family process of taking in a new member. Let them listen to the baby in the mother's tummy. Take them to the hospital where the baby will arrive. Perhaps you can show them the obstetric ward and the nursery. If parents take this approach, the older children are much less likely to feel excluded. Instead they will feel more grown-up and part of what everybody is going through. Most likely they will grasp the idea that there is plenty of love to go around, that they don't have to lose anything. One of the most important features of this approach is to have older children accompany the father when he goes to fetch the baby and the mother. Then everybody comes home together. Again, the other children are made participants in the big event.

But what if this approach doesn't work? What if one or more of the children react in one of two ways described earlier—showing anger and regression to babyhood themselves, or being so loving to the baby that everybody can see there is something phony about it?

One possible answer: don't act in a punitive way with the older child or children. It is easy to see why parents would feel like acting that way. They are tired, troubled, and busy with the new baby. They've done everything they can think of, and it doesn't seem to be working. So they get angry.

It is important for parents to realize that this is the most important time to tolerate a little hostility, overcompensation, or regression on the part of children who preceded the new arrival. Be patient with the way they try to make up for lowered self-esteem and a feeling of loss. Find ways to show them special attention, such as a party of their own, an extra hug or two, permission to watch an acceptable television program a little longer. When parents act in such ways, most children can very easily weather the coming of an addition to the family.

Depreciation and Rejection

Many children with depressive disorders whom we have studied have suffered depreciation or rejection by their parents or loved ones from birth onward, or at least over a period of many years. Rejection may take the form of blunt statements stressing the child's unworthiness or inadequacy, or it may be expressed more subtly through attitudes or actions that indicate a lack of respect, involvement, or caring. For instance, a parent may look at a child's report card, which contains high marks in some subjects and very low marks in others. The parent makes no comment at all. He or she simply signs the card and hands it back to the child.

In some cases the parent has subjected the child to a constant barrage of criticism and humiliation. In other cases there is simply a void in the parent-child relationship: the parent's love for the child is never expressed. Since the love often does exist, this is one of the most tragic situations that can occur in the relationship between parent and child.

Here we are talking about a whole range of human beings who are not very good at expressing loving feelings. They don't know how to say "I love you." They don't know how to express love around holiday time—or any other time—by sharing and giving. They don't have the ability to touch a child or an adult to show that they are caring.

Love in its essence consists not only of tenderness and caring but also of overt expressions of those feelings. There are many people who just can't do this. They aren't consciously doing anything bad. In their relations with other people they just have an emptiness they cannot fill. The result is particularly tragic for the children of such parents because to a child—or to a grown-up, for that matter—love is like sunshine and water to a plant. We see many children in therapy who have perfectly respectable parents. The parents really want to do the best they can. But they do not know how to express their love for the child. This is one of the hardest situations that a psychiatrist faces. Where a parent's love goes unexpressed, it may be necessary to find a relative or some other person who can supply the love the child needs. Possible candidates for such a task, in addition to relatives, are teachers, neighbors, scout masters, sports organizers or coaches, church leaders, and friends.

Sometimes the process of depreciation and rejection is related to a obvious characteristic of the child, such as a physical handicap. This most often occurs when the handicap is one that a parent has long been sensitive about. For example, the father may have only one testicle; if a son is born with the same condition, the father may shun him without realizing what he is doing, because he's embarrassed about his own situation and doesn't want a child who will feel as inadequate as he does. One of the fathers in the Cytryn study mentioned in Chapter One[4] who himself had an undescended testicle summed it up when talking about his son with the same condition, "Let's face it, he just doesn't have it."

This situation applies to many other conditions. If one parent is extremely short or extremely tall, or has long, stringy hair or is not particularly attractive, and if the unliked characteristic shows up in a child, that child may be shunned simply for having a trait the parent is embarrassed about. Sex, too, can rear its ugly head. A woman who hates being a woman will probably want only male children. If a daughter comes along, she may treat her quite badly. The child reminds her of herself and makes her feel bad, so she tends to ignore her. This doesn't always happen, and certainly not often. But in some cases it is the underlying reason for a poor parent-child relationship that can make the child feel disheartened and eventually push her into depression.

Depreciation of the child can be shown through overprotection as well as through rejection; both attitudes convey the same basic message of the child's inadequacy and worthlessness. Telling a boy, for example, that he should not use a certain playground because "a gang of bad kids" hangs out nearby is a reflection both on his state of knowledge and on his ability to look out for himself. How much of the child's depressive outlook is caused by identifying with this negative view of himself and how much is caused by a sense of alienation from important loved ones is often hard to determine. Some of these parental fears are obviously justified in neighborhoods where kidnapping and assaults on children are commonplace. In such situations a child is aware of the reality of the parents' warning and does not perceive it as overprotective.

Physical Stressors

Some depressed children have a physical disability. These patients include most importantly those enduring hospitalization, immobilization, pain, or disfigurement. Children with chronic disabilities—paralysis, kidney disease, severe allergies, heart disease—tend to have a chronic depression; the severity of such depressive condition depends on such factors as family background, personality, psychosocial stressors, and inherited biological makeup.[5]

Children of parents with a chronic physical illness often suffer episodes of depression either because of losing the parent through hospitalization or because of identifying with the parent's reaction to the physical illness.

Social Factors in Depressed Animals

The influence of social factors in depressive illness, and particularly the presence or absence of a good parent, is clearly seen in studies of nonhuman primate mothers and their offspring.

In the wild, young chimpanzees who have lost their mothers commonly develop depression. First they actively protest the loss. Then they show despair, become inactive, withdraw from social life, and develop apathy. Unless older siblings adopt these chimpanzee infants, the babies usually die within a few months. Because the female of the species is the primary caretaker of infants, investigators have focused their attention on the mother and child relationship. Studies of the father and child relationship in nonhuman and human species are still at the initial stage. The behavior of the deprived chimp infants is strikingly like that of deprived human infants as described by John Bowlby.[6]

Even more revealing than such observations in the wild are the experiments with rhesus monkeys conducted by psychologist Harry F. Harlow and his associates at the University of Wisconsin in the 1950s, 1960s, and 1970s.[7] The result of one of these experiments negates, or at least throws into question, the long-held notion that babies cling to the mother and thus start a life-long attachment to her simply because she offers them milk. Harlow separated newborn rhesus monkeys from their mothers shortly after birth and offered them substitute mothers. One of these substitutes was made of wood and covered with terry cloth. The other was made of wire and left uncovered. But this second substitute had one strong advantage—a nursing bottle filled with milk from which the baby could feed.

When a baby monkey was placed in a cage with the two substitutes, he made what at first glance may seem a surprising choice. He chose comfort rather than sustenance. He spent more time clinging to the soft terry-cloth substitute than he did climbing onto the wire creation and feeding from the bottle. There is a suggestion here that, at least in monkeys, physical closeness to a mother is more important even than being fed.

These monkeys raised apart from their mothers grew up to display odd sexual behavior (they felt the urge to procreate but did not know how). Moreover, the females, after they finally became pregnant, proved to be abusive and even murderous mothers. It may seem strange to anyone who has not watched a young child plead for attention, but the young monkeys that survived insisted on making contact with their abusive mothers—and on maintaining it. They did so in spite of strenuous and hurtful efforts by the mothers to keep them away. The result was sometimes surprising: eventually these mothers, worked upon by their infants' show of affection, began to be rehabilitated. They treated the babies and their later offspring much more effectively and warmly.

Ethologist R.A. Hinde[8] tested infant monkeys by placing them in a strange cage with strange objects. He found that the infants who had been separated from their mother—some for six days, some for thirteen—were fearful of the objects. They were less likely to approach them than animals who had been brought up with their mothers. This effect of separation lasted as long as two years. Other researchers separated infant monkeys from their mothers for only forty-eight hours. Even during such a short separation, all the babies showed signs of despair and protest.

Depression in children, as mentioned earlier, frequently stems from the loss of a "love object"—a person, place, or thing held very dear by the child. Something similar to this occurs in monkeys, too. A student of Harlow's, Stephen J. Soumi,[9] raised pairs of infant monkeys together and then separated them. The result was profound melancholy, fright, and withdrawal. At ninety days, when the monkeys should have started to play, they remained sad, aloof, infantlike. As they grew older they remained fixated at the ninety-day stage of development.

Earlier research had suggested that monkeys deprived of affection for as long as six months had been emotionally destroyed. But Soumi took these depressed animals and placed them in pairs with animals three months younger—at just the age when they were starting to play. In other words, he gave each depressed monkey a model of normal behavior. The results were surprising. The depressed animals gradually became more outgoing, accepted approaches, and began making approaches themselves. Before long they were engaging in uninhibited play. So far as anyone could tell, they were normal. Whether similar therapy would work with humans is not known.

Soumi reviewed his research on the results of separation of infant monkeys from their mothers.[10] Most of the monkeys respond to the initial moments of separation with fear, resembling a human panic attack. These anxious reactions can last over prolonged periods of time. There is a variety of environmental factors that increase the chance a monkey will respond to separation in this way and increase its intensity, in particular, early frequent separation from mother, ill treatment at the hands of an abusive mother, and frequent changes in the social group around the infant. If you study traumatic separation from mother in adolescent monkeys, you find a very different reaction, a prolonged period of agitated activity. So one sees a very different response to the same stress in an animal in a different developmental phase.

Despite the developmentally different responses to separation, the underlying physiological response to this stress, as seen in certain measures, is the same in infant, adolescent, and adult monkeys, namely, an increase in plasma cortisol levels. This, by the way, corresponds to the human response to stress.

Although most monkeys respond in these developmentally and physiologically predictable ways, there are striking individual differences which must be taken into account if the stress is somewhat less intense. While some monkeys show the various fearful responses noted above, others reared in similar backgrounds respond to stress with playful and exploratory behavior.[11] Thus, there would appear to be "anxiety-prone" and "timid" monkeys and another group of "outgoing" monkeys. The differences between these two groups of monkeys are stable over time and are reflected in their cortisol levels, which are high for the anxious monkeys and low for the curious ones.

It seems that infant, adolescent, and adult monkeys respond to stress in developmentally predictable ways, with certain crucial individual differences. What happens when these brief separations are prolonged? The initial anxiety responses are followed by the appearance of "depression," i.e., social isolation, low activity levels, and disruption in eating and sleeping. Animals that don't show the fearful reaction to separation don't develop this "depressive" picture.

An interesting phenomenon occurs when "outgoing" infant monkeys are separated but can still see their mother.[12] They respond with high levels of vocalization—in common parlance, they put up a fuss, much more so than their more anxious peers. It can be argued that such a fuss is very adaptive in the jungle, where mother needs to know quickly if one of her group has wandered off. It is certainly more adaptive than the fearful-depressive response of the "timid" monkeys, who are at high risk for developing permanent depressive patterns. These differences would appear to be both environmental and hereditary. Soumi summarizes by commenting that "high stress reactivity" seems to be a "highly heritable trait characteristic."

Recently, Soumi elaborated on the feasibility of using primates as models for human depression.[13] Rhesus monkeys share ninety-four percent of the genetic material with humans, making behavioral and physiological comparisons useful. Obviously, one can manipulate the monkey's social environment in ways that would not be acceptable in human research. Although the depressive symptoms in monkeys are only approximate equivalents of depressive disorders in humans, the two species have many things in common. Like depressed humans, bereaved monkeys show elevated cortisol levels, as well as a decrease in socialization and general functioning. In addition, the depressive symptoms in monkeys respond to antidepressant medications such as imipramine and the newer SSRIs, with a delay of ten to fourteen days, closely paralleling human response to such medication. Finally, rhesus monkeys respond just like humans to the dexamethasone suppression test.

There was one famous study of human infants that parallels Soumi's previously mentioned therapy of monkeys who became depressed after separation. In this study, children were taken from an orphanage, where the environment was unstimulating and they received only minimal attention, and placed in the care of women living in a home for the mentally retarded.[14] There were thirteen such children, with an average IQ of 64. The retarded women adored them and gave them considerable attention. In two years the children's average IQ rose to normal levels, and they went on to live productive adult lives. The average IQ of twelve children who remained in the unstimulating orphanage dropped 26 points in two years and as adults they lived in the main unproductively.

Why the difference? One answer seems to be that the nature of the social environment after the separation takes place has a deep influence on the infant's reaction. For instance, where socially interested adult caretakers are present, the infant appears less likely to be upset.

Telemetering Information from the Monkey

Martin Reite[15] of the University of Colorado Medical Center points out that the higher primates, more closely than nonprimates, resemble humans in two important ways—the structure of the central nervous system and the richness and variability of behavior. Lower animals operate on simple reflexes, or on a simple group of behaviors geared to a given situation; they do not have the wide repertoire available to humans and monkeys.

To facilitate the study of behavior and physiology in young monkeys, Reite's laboratory developed a telemetry system that can be implanted in the monkey's body and that sends back information on body temperature, heart rate, eye movement, muscle activity, and three measurements of the brain waves. Because of this development, information about the monkey's physiology can be obtained while the animal is engaged in normal activities unrestrained. In addition, the animal's behavior is videotaped.

Reite's research team has studied twenty infant monkeys. Telemetry units were implanted in them when they were five or six months old, and the units were turned on after they had recovered from surgery. The investigators recorded baseline observations for several days; then they separated the mother and the young offspring, half for four days and half for ten days. Immediately after separation, the baby monkeys began behaving in an agitated manner and their heart rates shot up. Their heart rates remained above normal through most of the first day of separation and then began dropping. As the separation continued, there was a tendency for the heart rate to return toward normal.

Sleep habits changed markedly the first night of separation. The animals spent more time awake, awoke more often, and spent considerably less time in so-called REM (for rapid eye movement) sleep. In REM sleep the eyeballs move constantly though the eyes are closed. It is known that in humans during such periods the sleeper is dreaming. As separation continued, most of the monkeys returned to their normal patterns, but REM periods remained abnormal until they were reunited with the mother.

Like heart rate, body temperature rose during the period of agitated behavior, which continued through much of the first night. This was followed by depressed behavior, which continued throughout the separation. The levels returned to normal following reunion with the mother.

Odd though it may seem, experiments performed with mongrel dogs over twenty-five years ago by Martin E. P. Seligman of the University of Pennsylvania led to a new idea about the nature and treatment of childhood depression. In 1967, Seligman and coworkers exposed dogs to uncontrollable electric shocks. Then they put each animal in a two-compartment cage, where the shocks could be controlled. All the animal had to do when shock was applied was to jump from one compartment to the other. In the second compartment he was safe. But most dogs, probably because of their previous inability to escape the shocks, just lay passively and took shock after shock without a whimper. They failed to learn how they could escape by simply jumping over a low barrier. The researchers described the dog's attitude as learned helplessness.[16] The animals had learned, during the first phase of the experiment, that nothing they could do would put an end to their misery. When conditions were changed so that they could do something, the initial lesson remained and they made no attempt to escape.

Seligman has since argued that there are strikingly similar parallels between helplessness and human depression. He proposes that the inability to control a bad situation or event leads some people to an expectation of helplessness and that this expectation leads to odd or abnormal behavior and eventually to depression. But the extent of such behavior depends upon the "causal attributions" people make about the uncontrollable events—in other words, how they account for the events that trouble them.

Does an individual believe that the uncontrollable events are caused by something within himself, by his own characteristics? In other words, does he think that he himself is responsible? In that case, the causal attribution—or the reason the person gives for a bad event—is described as *internal*. If the individual attributes the uncontrollable events to factors that persist over time, the attribution is described as *stable*. Finally, if the individual attributes the uncontrollable events to causes present in a variety of situations, not in just one or two, the attribution is described as *global*.

According to Seligman,[17]

> To the degree that a person points to internal, stable, and global causes of bad events, then that person is increasingly likely to be helpless and depressed once a bad event is encountered. Depression (in children and adults) results from characteristics of an individual (i.e., the "depressive" attributional style) in conjunction with characteristics of the environment (i.e., uncontrollable bad events). Neither the attributional style nor the uncontrollable events alone result in widespread helplessness and depression; only their co-occurrence leads to depression.

How does a child acquire his attributional style or the characteristic way he or she explains events that markedly affect his or her life? Seligman attempted to throw light on this question by comparing the styles of eighty parents with those of their offspring.[18] He found that a mother's attributional style for bad events correlated with both her child's attributional style for bad events and her child's depressive symptoms. The father's attributional style, however, was not related to the styles of his children or of his mate, apparently because much of his life was lived separately. "The child may learn attributional style (or depressive symptoms) from its mother," Seligman speculates, "and then the depressions of mother and child may maintain each other. . . ."

If a maladaptive attributional style leads to depression, can the style be changed? As a major part of his continuing research, Seligman has demonstrated that it can. In a preliminary study, his subjects were twenty depressed children who believed that bad events in their life were caused by their own behavior. Seligman tried to help these children to see that they did not have to blame themselves and that a bad situation need not endure but can often be changed—in short, that their thinking was fallacious regarding the causes of their disorder. Seligman reported that, with his treatment methods, some 80 percent of these depressed children improved remarkably, and that their improvement has continued through the first six months he has followed them.[17,18]

Nature of the Biological Abnormality

If a predisposition or a tendency to develop a major depressive illness is inherited, as it seems to be in a great many cases, the question of *what* is inherited becomes important. Something could have gone awry in some of the billions of neurons that constitute the brain's gray matter, or in the functioning of some other part of the body, or in the way certain parts of the brain or the rest of the body interact.

In the last two decades, there has been a virtual explosion of new information about the way the neurons (cells of the central nervous system) communicate. The present, highly vaunted "Decade of the Brain," is a culmination of the most exciting developments in neuroscience, propelled mainly by advances in cell and molecular biology. These, in turn, have been aided by sophisticated imaging technologies, which enable scientists to visualize and quantify transmitter and drug receptors, enzymes, and other parts of the nerve cells, including their transmitting machinery.[19] As a result, the direct study of the function of the nervous system at the molecular level is replacing the older, indirect, and largely hypothetical methods of inquiry.[20]

Human communication involves the use of words to convey the basic content of its message, which is modulated by nonverbal means, such as the tone of voice, facial expression, and body movements. The communication between two neurons involves the use of chemical messengers, neurotransmitters, to convey the content of their information. While human verbal interaction is usually bidirectional, the neural flow of information is unidirectional, always proceeding from the sending neuron, across a narrow divide, called a synapsis or synaptic cleft, to the receiving neuron. The former is called the presynaptic neuron, and the latter is the postsynaptic neuron. The electrical impulse in the presynaptic neuron releases its neurotransmitter, which is stored in vesicles located in the nerve endings, into the synaptic cleft, where it attaches itself to specialized protein receptors.

As our knowledge has expanded, scientists have become aware of the complexity of this flow of messages coursing through the dense neural network. The immensely diverse intervening steps in this communication are akin to relays and switches in modern voice and image transmission. It is precisely this diversity that allows for the most subtle modulation of the interneuronal communication,[21] similar to the nonverbal modulation of human conversation. It would be beyond the scope of this book to present this process in great detail. However, we will attempt to describe some of its essential components.

Neurotransmitters

More than 30 neurotransmitters have been identified in the central nervous system to date. Presumably they may all play a role in regulation of behavior and psychiatric illness. Three of these neurotransmitters, namely, *dopamine, norepinephrine,* and *serotonin,* have been studied more intensively in psychiatry than others, because of their possible implication in depression, as well as in a host of other psychiatric disorders.

Thanks to ingenious and persistent efforts of numerous investigators, our knowledge of these neurotransmitters has become much more sophisticated and complex. Various studies have provided bits of knowledge which gradually fit into a comprehensive roadmap, providing information about the origin and distribution of these neurotransmitters, the many safeguards regulating their availability at the synapse, and how they interact with each other in order to maintain the balance necessary for optimal functioning of the system.

The neurotransmitters originate in specific cell bodies located in various areas of the brain (the midbrain, pons, and brainstem). From there, structures of the nerve cell that conduct nervous impulses away from the cell body (axon) project to virtually all areas of the brain, like wires in a dense telephone system. Many of these areas are reached by all three neurotransmitter systems, which often interconnect and interact with each other. It is believed that such interaction may be essential to the regulation of normal behavior, and that its malfunction is at the root of psychiatric illness.

Such an integrative approach is gradually replacing our previous single neurotransmitter hypotheses of depression and other mental disorders, while leaving open the possibility that in some types or subtypes of psychiatric disorders (such as mania) the activity of one specific neurotransmitter may play a predominant role.[22]

Receptors

Langley, in 1905, was the first to suggest: (1) that protein receptor substances exist in cells, and (2) that neurotransmitters, drugs, and hormones exert their biological function by interacting with these receptors. In time, specific receptors were isolated and identified for all neurotransmitters, as well as for other substances (hormones, peptides, amino acids) and for drugs. Many substances have several receptors, each acting independently and activating a different function. Of the three neurotransmitters implicated in affective disorders, it is now known that norepinephrine has at least four receptors, serotonin at least seven, and dopamine two. New receptors are being identified at a very fast pace.

The process of receptor functioning has been gradually clarified: (1) A biological substance (neurotransmitter, hormone, or drug) binds to an appropriate receptor; (2) an adjacent protein known as an effector is mobilized; (3) the effector activates one or more of the following: (a) transfer of ions or molecules, (b) enzyme activation or deactivation, (c) protein synthesis, (d) release of hormones or transmitters; and (4) a specific biological response occurs, which could be moving your hand, solving a puzzle or altering your mood.[23]

Synaptic Transmission

As late as twenty years ago, it was believed that the process of synaptic transmission was rather simple, in that a transmitter released in a presynaptic neuron directly influenced the postsynaptic neuronal cell. Recently, a more sophisticated picture has emerged of many possible "variations on the theme," with modulation occurring in either the presynaptic or postsynaptic receptors (embedded in the respective end-membranes of two adjacent neurons).[22]

The transmitter molecules have specialized shapes, which allow them to lock onto their receptors, literally fitting together like pieces of a puzzle.

There may be more neurotransmitter molecules released by the neuron into the synaptic gap than there are available receptors. This excess is either destroyed by an enzyme, called monoamine oxidase (MAO), or is drawn back into its vesicle on the presynaptic neuron and deactivated during the process of reuptake. As mentioned previously, the presynaptic receptors give the necessary feedback about the amount of the released neurotransmitter and thus regulate the process of its production and utilization according to the demands of the interneuronal communication. The flexibility of synaptic transmission is further enhanced by an ingenious ability of the postsynaptic neuron to increase the number of its receptors when not enough of the neurotransmitter is available, and conversely, to decrease the number of receptors when a neurotransmitter surplus exists. In affective disorders, such modulation is believed to be malfunctioning or insufficient.

Some mention, however brief, should be made about our current concepts of the nature of postsynaptic receptors.[24] Many receptors are grouped into two large families, based on common characteristics. The members of the first one are linked to *ion channels,* which function like gates through which small inorganic ions like calcium, sodium, potassium, and chloride simply flow from one side of the neuronal membrane to the other, altering in the process the electrical activity of nerve cells. The members of the second large family of receptors are linked to enzymes that produce intracellular structures called *second messengers.* These can lead to long-lasting metabolic effects in their postsynaptic targets (usually by regulating the phosphorylation of specific protein substrates). The second messenger system is very complex and, in fact, not yet fully elucidated.

The above rather cursory overview of the current knowledge of the interneuronal communication, with its rich modulatory capabilities, should help explain the wonderful plasticity of the central nervous system and its ability to maintain internal equilibrium and control of our emotional states, except when overwhelmed by a pathological process beyond its regulatory capacity.

Some Other Biological Effects

There are a number of biological abnormalities that accompany depressive states. It is very important for us to know whether these are *state* or *trait* abnormalities. A state abnormality would be one that occurred just during depressive episodes, while a trait abnormality would occur throughout the person's lifetime, or much of the person's lifetime, and would be present before, during, and after any particular depressive episode.

State and trait markers are extremely important, both theoretically and practically, in dealing with depressive disorders. Theoretically, one is concerned with the issue of continuity versus discontinuity in depressive illness; that is to say, is the child's illness the same as the adult illness? These markers also have practical implications, since we want to know if the depressive disorder seen in a child is likely to recur in adulthood. But the most immediate practical issue is: can we use trait markers to identify people who are risk for the illness long before it ever occurs, so that preventive measures can be taken?

State markers are important in cases where it may be difficult to make a diagnosis on the basis of clinical symptoms alone. There are several common state markers of mood disorders in adults, among them changes in blood cortisol and growth hormone levels, dexamethasone suppression test (DST), urinary excretion of the cathecholamine metabolite 3-methoxy-4-hydroxyphenyl-ethylene glycol (MHPG), sleep EEG and sleep disturbances. Some of them either appear full-blown or have early precursors in children and adolescents with affective disorders.

Depression is associated with a variety of sleep disturbances. One of them is a shortening of the period between the time a person goes to sleep and the time he begins dreaming, or the onset of rapid eye movements (REM) sleep. Others are decreased slow-wave sleep, increased frequency of REM sleep, and decreased sleep efficiency. Depressed latency-aged children do not show the variable EEG patterns seen in adults. There is strong evidence that age has a fundamental influence on sleep EEG; consequently, developmental differences between children and adults would seem to explain why depressed children do not show sleep EEG changes. As put by Dr. Joachim Puig-Antich, "Negative sleep findings in prepubertal major depressives may be explained by maturational differences in the nature of sleep."[25,26]

Confirmation of this idea is beginning to emerge from the study of adolescent depressives. The sleep disturbances noted in adults begin to become evident as depressives enter adolescence, which is accompanied by increasing brain maturation. REM latency only becomes abnormal in late adolescence, while abnormalities in sleep continuity become evident very early in adolescence. So one sees a broad range of time-correlated onsets of the sleep difficulties seen in adults.[25]

Another common biochemical abnormality during depression is the increased secretion of cortisol, a hormone produced by the adrenal glands and associated with stress.[27] In addition, if dexamethasone (a chemical which suppresses the activity of the adrenal glands) is given, many adult depressives will still hyper-secrete cortisol.[28] These changes in cortisol are state-dependent; that is, cortisol production and secretion return to normal levels when the person is no longer depressed. Cortisol hypersecretion is found much less frequently in latency-aged children with major depression than in depressed adults. The majority of children have normal cortisol secretion both during and after a major depressive episode.

Again, as with the EEG, age seems to govern this process.[29] The older patients are, the more likely they are to hypersecrete cortisol when they have a depressed period, whether they are children or adults. Puig-Antich found a very low rate of dexamethasone nonsuppression among both prepubertal children with depression and normal children.[25] However, as depressed adolescents mature into adulthood, they increasingly show the full adult picture of dexamethasone nonsuppression.[30]

Growth hormone secretion has also been extensively studied in adults. When challenged by a variety of pharmacological agents, such as insulin, dextroamphetamine, desimipramine, and clonidine, normal adults respond with increased blood levels of growth hormone, indicating its release from the pituitary gland. Depressed adults, on the other hand, show a blunted growth hormone stimulation, i.e., hyposecretion, when given the same stimulating agents.[31,32]

Depressed latency-aged children have shown the same blunted response (hyposecretion) of growth hormone in response to insulin-induced hypoglycemia as is seen in adults.[25,33,34] Another interesting finding is that growth hormone abnormalities persist even when the child's mood returns to normal. This raises the possibility that growth hormone is a trait marker for latency-aged children with major depression.[25]

In other research, we examined urinary norepinephrine metabolites in chronically depressed children and found that they excreted significantly less 3-methoxy-4-hydroxyphenyl-ethylene glycol (MHPG) in twenty-four hours than normal controls,[35,36] paralleling the findings in adults.[37] We also found that children with a bipolar disorder had a strongly augmented EEG average evoked response (AER) to sensory stimuli,[38] again paralleling findings in adults.[39] However, the alteration in the MHPG urinary excretion, as well as that of the AER, have to be considered *state* markers, since they return to normal once the child has recovered.

The Genetic Risk

Unless you are a close relative—meaning a parent, a brother or sister, or a son or daughter—of a person with a major, unipolar, or bipolar depression, you have less than one chance in ten of developing the disease yourself. If you are a close relative of such a patient, you have about a 25 to 30 percent chance of developing the condition sometime in your lifetime. However, when both parents have a major affective illness, the chances of a child's developing a major mood disorder rise to about 70 percent.

Studies of twins have proven very useful in clarifying the role of genetic factors in many illnesses. Identical (monozygotic) twins develop from the same fertilized egg and therefore share all their genes. On the other hand, nonidentical (dizygotic) twins develop from two separate fertilized eggs and only share about 50 percent of their genes, just like ordinary siblings. As a result, one would expect that identical twins would more often share a hereditary illness than nonidentical twins. This has proven to be the case in many medical and psychiatric disorders, including schizophrenia, autism, Alzheimer's disease, and some forms of profound mental retardation (fragile X syndrome). Twin studies in major affective disorders indicate that if one identical twin develops a major affective illness, the other twin is affected as well in about 50 percent of the cases, while such concordance in nonidentical twins reaches only about 25 percent.[40]

The study of adopted children represents another important method of ascertaining the relative importance of genetic environmental factors in affective disorders. One of the early pioneers in studying adopted children, David Rosenthal, looked at several hundred adopted young people.[41] Some of these were

children of a parent with a manic-depressive (bipolar) or schizophrenic illness who had been given up for adoption at an early
age. Others were adopted people whose biological parents were
free of major psychiatric illness. A third group was comprised of
children whose own parents were mentally healthy but who had
been adopted and raised by couples, one of whom was either
manic-depressive or schizophrenic.

The gist of Rosenthal's findings was that, in the transmission
of manic-depressive disorder and schizophrenia, heredity counts
more than the parent-child relationship or, by implication, environment in general. Other adoption studies, notably that of Sey-
mour Kety and his group,[42] demonstrated a significant genetic
contribution to unipolar depression and suicide.

The numerous twin and adoption studies carried out in the
last half-century offer ample evidence that a genetic predisposition exists in a substantial proportion of patients with manic-
depressive illness and major depression. However, many issues
in the field of genetic studies remain unsettled. One of them
concerns the relationship of unipolar to bipolar illness. Some see
the subtypes of affective disorders existing on a continuum of
severity; this is the position proposed by Elliot Gershon at the
National Institute of Mental Health. Others contend that the subtypes represent discrete genetic entities, independently trans-
mitted. This controversy is related to another unresolved issue—
whether one or several genes are involved in the transmission of
affective illness. Ongoing, fruitful genetic research holds out the
promise of further clarification and eventual resolution of the
remaining mysteries surrounding the hereditary aspects of
mood disorders.[43]

In sum, depression at any age may be the result of social or
biological factors or both. Social factors include either loss of or
rejection by a loved one. Rejection doesn't necessarily mean that
the child is actually ignored or pushed out of the loved one's life.
It can also mean that someone simply fails to give him the warm
attention and love that he needs for his best development. A
family whose members are abnormally close to one another and

fearful of the world outside can foster depression in a youngster. So can families who set goals too high for their child. Depression may be associated, too, with a physiological disability suffered either by a child or a parent. Underlying all of these causes of childhood depression, there is likely to be a disorder in the child's biological makeup something that is inherited and thus makes the child predisposed to depression.

SIX

Who Is at Risk?

As reported in the November 1992 issue of *Psychiatric News*, Tony Dow, the actor who played Wally Cleaver on the popular television show "Leave It to Beaver," told members of Congress that depression brought him to the brink of suicide, and treatment saved his life.

Dow said, "People with depression are regular people, I mean, who could be more regular than Wally Cleaver?"

Nobody is cheerful all of the time. Everybody goes through low periods, when he or she takes a gloomy view of what's going on, wonders whether the sun will ever shine again, questions whether there are any really good things in life—and if there are, whether he or she can ever attain them.

In that sense, everybody is at risk for depressive moods and such moods are ubiquitous. Unless caused by the loss of a loved one, or a move from loved surroundings, they rarely last more than a week, if that. And even when they have been occasioned by a deeply felt loss, they rarely linger more than a few months.

What we are dealing with throughout this book is depression that persists or is recurrent—the kind that interferes with a child's functioning, with eating and sleeping, play, school and social activities, and/or conduct, rather than a stage through which the child is passing or a transient change of mood. It is more serious and pervasive—something that the child does not seem to be able to shake without assistance.

Being at risk means that your probability of being afflicted by a given condition is greater than it is in the general population. People may be at risk for mental illness because the condition runs in their families and they have inherited a genetic predisposition to it. They can also be at risk because they were raised in a dysfunctional family or subjected to severe life circumstances.

Children with a Depressed Parent

As mentioned earlier, the children most at risk for major depressive illness are those whose parent has a major affective illness. The risk involves both genetic and psychosocial factors and "is among the largest risk factors for depression across the life span."[1]

Geneticist Elliot Gershon and his associates at the National Institute of Mental Health (NIMH) examined five hundred and twenty-four first-degree relatives (direct blood relatives) of people in Israel diagnosed with psychotic depression.[2] Of these relatives, forty-nine had some form of major depressive illness, as compared with only four relatives of six hundred and nineteen normal controls. In other words, there was about ten times as much serious depressive illness within families containing some depressed people as within families without such depressed members. Moreover, depressed patients had about eight times as many relatives with dysthymic disorder or with so-called cyclothymic disorder, in which periods of moderate depression and moderate elation occur regardless of what's going on outside the affected person.

Some years ago we studied thirty children,[3] aged five to fifteen, of fifteen adult patients who had been hospitalized for either unipolar or bipolar illness. We saw the children twice, four months apart. Of fourteen boys, five were diagnosed as depressed both times we saw them, and three were diagnosed only once as depressed. Of the sixteen girls, four were diagnosed both times as depressed, eleven only one time. Thus, roughly one-third of the children who had a parent hospitalized for affective illness were themselves rated depressed.

A further study using the same methods brought similar results.[4] But this time the conclusions could be firmer because the study included not only school-aged children of affectively ill parents but also controls, that is, children whose parents were emotionally well. Of the thirteen families in which at least one parent had a major affective illness, eleven had one or more children who were depressed on at least one interview. In contrast, of the thirteen control families only three had children who were depressed at any time. The fact that children who have at least one parent with a major affective illness are at greater risk for a mood disorder has been further confirmed by numerous investigators whose findings have been recently reviewed.[5] The well-known phenomenon of assortative mating (i.e., the tendency of people to marry people with the same or similar characteristics) means that there is an increased risk of an affective illness in the spouse of a depressed parent. Obviously, the psychosocial and genetic risk to the child in such cases is greatly increased.[1]

Age is an important variable of this risk, as described at length in Chapter Three. Infants, toddlers, and preschool children of affectively ill parents rarely develop depression and usually only under the most adverse circumstances. The risk increases with age, with the rate of depression in the offspring of a parent with mood disorder reaching as high as 30 percent by the end of adolescence.[6]

In studies of psychosocial factors in the offspring of parents with depressive illness, two have received the most attention: (1) interference of the disorder with the ability to parent, and (2) the presence of severe marital discord and divorce.[7,8]

It should be mentioned that most of the depressed children in our second study[4] had a chronic form of the illness (dysthymic rather than a major depressive disorder). None was psychotic, and none had symptoms of mania or hypomania, although thirteen of the fifteen parents were bipolar. However, it should be stressed that several recent follow-up studies indicate that many children with unipolar depression go on the develop a bipolar disorder later in life.[9] In addition, many children with dysthymic disorder consequently develop major depressive disorder.[10]

Eighteen of the children seen in our first study continued to be followed. At the time of the original study, the mean age of the children was ten years; at the time of the follow-up study, their mean age was fourteen years. To interview them we chose investigators who did not know how either the children or the parents had been previously diagnosed. As in the previous studies, each child was interviewed twice, four months apart.

Originally, twelve of the eighteen youngsters had been diagnosed as depressed on either one or both of the two interviews. At follow-up seven of those were depressed on one or both of the interviews; of the remaining five, three had some type of psychiatric disorder (overanxious disorder, conduct disorder, or obsessive-compulsive disorder). Only two of the children rated depressed at the time of the first study were considered free of any psychiatric disorder at follow-up. Of the six youngsters not originally diagnosed as depressed, five were considered free of psychopathology at follow-up and only one had a major depression.

In conclusion, our study indicates that, if untreated, children who are significantly depressed have an unfavorable prognosis, at least in adolescence.[11] Almost half of the children we studied were depressed on follow-up, and most of the remainder went on to develop a variety of other nondepressive emotional disorders. The hopeful note is that most of the children who were free of depression in childhood continued to enjoy relatively good mental health during adolescence. Because of the consistency over time of the psychopathology or its absence, it seems of paramount importance that childhood depression be taken with utmost seriousness and be vigorously treated.

In a similar study, Elva Poznanski and her colleagues interviewed ten children aged twelve to twenty-three who had been diagnosed as depressed six and a half years earlier.[12] They found that 50 percent of these children were clinically depressed at follow-up and that none of the remainder was free of psychopathology.

Because children of parents with affective illness represent a group clearly at risk, any psychiatrist or other therapist evaluating or treating such *adults* should inquire about the emotional status of their children. We have often found a family interview, including all family members, to be revealing. Moreover, all mental health practitioners, when seeing depressed *children,* should inquire about the possible existence of a similar disorder in the siblings or parents.

We should like to emphasize that by no means do all children of depressed parents become depressed. Though they are said to be at risk for depression, many live completely normal lives. It is reasonable to describe some of these children as invulnerable.

Invulnerable Children

The concept of invulnerability has received considerable attention among investigators of schizophrenia.[13] For example, psychiatrist E. James Anthony has pointed out that when an invulnerable child turns up in a family with a schizophrenic parent, he or she is likely to have had little contact with the ill parent for whatever reason. Such a situation allows the child to avoid over-identification with the sick parent.

The child who is likely to develop a schizophrenic illness, according to Anthony and his associates, is the child who is close to the sick parent. This child often acts as a caretaker of the parent and, by doing so, seems to hasten the process of identifying with her or him. Anthony tells of a family whose schizophrenic mother would never eat at home because she feared someone was poisoning the food. The father and son would not accompany her to restaurants because they did not share her belief. Though the daughter may have been skeptical, she humored her mother and ate wherever she ate. The son stayed well. The daughter, after entering college, began showing signs of schizophrenia, the result perhaps of genetic influences as well as those factors described above.

The same process seems to be at work with affective disorders. We first noticed this when we were seeing the families of the depressed children under our care. If one of the parents was depressed, the child we were treating often was emotionally close to that parent. In a family interview, the child would sit next to that parent, often clinging to him or her, in many cases looking quite as depressed as the depressed adult, upon whom the child was very dependent, but at the same time made special efforts to protect.

We realize that the above findings may cause considerable concern among readers who have an affective illness and worry about their offspring. It is important to keep in mind that at least 70 percent of the children of depressed parents do not develop depression, even in adolescence. Furthermore, most affective disorders are episodic in nature, and people with even major disorders can expect lengthy periods of good emotional health. During such healthy periods most affectively disturbed people function well and often are unusually warm and empathic. This latter circumstance can go a long way toward compensating for difficulties encountered during the periods of illness. In addition, we believe that the impressive progress in treatment possibilities may prevent recurrences.

Hyperactive Children May Also Be Depressed

Attention deficit hyperactivity disorder (ADHD) seems to be a high risk for a depressive illness. Typically, these children cannot remain quiet. They are often marked by restless and aggressive behavior, difficulty in concentrating, problems in doing schoolwork, clumsiness, and learning disabilities. Some have signs of minor neurological impairment that would account for many of their behavioral difficulties. The typical attention deficit hyperactivity disorder child is into everything. Some are involved in antisocial activity, such as stealing, truancy, or generally acting out. Usually, these children cause distress at home and in school by their continual restlessness and inability to concentrate.

At least some of these children are now believed to be depressed. They often rank low in self-esteem and feel worthless and helpless, unable to control their lives, and isolated from their peers. These symptoms are generally shared by depressed children. Walid Shekim reported that 30 percent of children with attention deficit hyperactivity disorder were also diagnosed as depressed.[14]

The relationship of ADHD to depression in children is not yet fully clarified. Among the two most likely possibilities are: (1) that hyperactive children develop a secondary reactive depression in response to the many hardships incurred by their illness (school failure, lack of friends, family conflicts, disappointments); and (2) that hyperactivity and depression have a parallel etiology and coexist in the same child as autonomous entities.[15]

Delinquency and Depression

Javad Kashani, in collaboration with us, studied one hundred boys and girls aged eleven to seventeen who had been incarcerated by the court in a juvenile justice center in central Missouri.[16] Of these, almost one-third had a depressive disorder, the most common symptoms being a feeling of sadness or unhappiness, sleep disorders, and changes in appetite. The girls exhibited a much higher incidence of depression than the boys. When examined prior to being committed to the institution, however, the youngsters had a similar rate of depression as seen in normal populations. There are two theories to explain the sudden and drastic change. The more obvious one is that life in a juvenile justice center is not exactly a happy experience. The other possible explanation is that the delinquents' capacity to act out their impulses had been taken away by the structure of the institutional environment. Many youngsters can't stand losing this capacity and defend against this loss of freedom by becoming depressed.

Recently, much attention has been paid to the impact of physical and sexual abuse of children. It has been demonstrated that such maltreatment often leads to a variety of psychiatric disorders, particularly affective disorder and delinquency.[17]

The Sex Factor in Depression

The majority of studies reports a higher rate of depressive symptoms in women than in men,[18,22] with an average female to male ratio of two to one. This sex ratio exists in unipolar disorders, but almost equal numbers of men and women suffer from bipolar (manic-depressive) disorders.[23] The explanations offered for the greater susceptibility of women to depression[22] include endocrine factors, higher reactivity to stress, and an inferior social status resulting in greater passivity and dependency.

The one-month prevalence of mental disorders in the United States, estimated by the National Institute of Mental Health Epidemiologic Catchment Area Program, indicates that men have higher rates of alcohol and substance abuse and antisocial personality, whereas women have higher rates of affective, anxiety, and somatization disorders. For affective disorders only, the rate for women of all ages is 6.6 percent. Moreover, affective disorders have been found in women at twice the rate as in men in international surveys in London, Australia, and Athens.[24]

During childhood, the incidence of depressive disorders of any type is equally distributed among boys and girls. The rates for unipolar disorders for females gradually increases during adolescence. As mentioned before, bipolar disorders affect males and females in equal numbers throughout life.

Sociodemographic Factors

Much more mental illness occurs among poor people than among those who make up the middle and upper classes. There are more schizophrenics among poor people, more depressed people, and more manic-depressives; in fact, almost all diseases (physical and mental) show up with greater frequency among poor people than among the wealthy. In a follow-up study in an Epidemiologic Catchment Area (ECA), poverty was shown to be a significant risk factor for depression.[25]

The reasons for more illness among the poor are most likely

environmental. Poor people have to contend not only with poorer housing, clothing, and food but also with poorer medical care. They have less access to services for their babies, both before and after childbirth. The person born into a poverty-stricken environment has less opportunity to rise and in many respects must struggle harder than his/her opposite number in the better-off classes simply to live. An extensive study of close to seven thousand Alameda County residents indicates that low education, poor perceived health, a strong sense of personal uncertainty, job loss, financial problems, family instability, a sense of anomie and social isolation were all associated with increased risk for depressive symptoms.[26] Moreover, well-educated persons from financially secure backgrounds are more likely than those from poor and minority groups to admit to emotional troubles and get psychiatric and/or medical help in time for it to do the most good.[27]

Other Groups at Risk for Depression

In Chapter One, we indicated that the impetus for one author's study of childhood depression was the frequent finding of depressive symptoms in chronically ill and handicapped children. Such findings have since been confirmed by many psychiatric and pediatric investigators.[28] In addition to the conditions previously named as existing concomitant with depression, others have been added, such as epilepsy, burns, asthma, diabetes, colitis, and leukemia and other forms of cancer. It stands to reason that the depressive states and other forms of psychopathology seen in these groups (anxiety, acting-out behavior) are a reaction to a difficult or hopeless life situation.

Another group neglected in terms of their feelings are the mentally retarded. It is true that the severely retarded are very difficult to assess psychologically; however, among the majority, who are only mildly retarded, there are many, especially during adolescence, who develop depressive symptoms and even a depressive disorder, which may seriously compound their already marginal functioning.[29]

Childhood depression is far from being completely under-stood, but we do know many factors that seem to be instrumental in its etiology. The most important is the presence of a parent or other close relative who is afflicted with a major affective illness. A predisposition to this illness can be genetically passed on to the child. Exactly what biological process is responsible for the predisposition is not yet known, but it may lie dormant in the child unless spurred to life by some source of stress in the child's environment—grief over the loss of a loved person or thing or any of a number of other traumatic factors discussed in Chapter Two. It is still a matter of debate whether the gene can become expressive without environmental stress. Remember, most children with depressed parents do *not* themselves become depressed.

The most hopeful note on the influence of parental depression on children is that drugs continue to be developed to check depression and allow the parents to function well, particularly if the medication is accompanied by psychotherapy.

Our work and the work of others suggest that a sizable proportion of depressed children, if untreated, remain depressed through adolescence. Frequently, this takes the form of chronic depression (dysthymic disorder). Other children may go through quiescent periods interspersed with depressive relapses, while others develop an early bipolar illness. Children with major physical as well as emotional handicaps are more likely than normal children to be depressed.

We have been talking throughout this chapter of children who are at risk for depressive illness. But being at risk does not mean that a child who happens to be vulnerable is bound to develop depression. It only means that his chances of doing so are greater than average.

Protective Factors

We mentioned previously in this chapter the concept of invulnerability, i.e., the fact that most children of depressed parents do not develop psychopathogy, including depression, and are functioning reasonably well. This resilience has been investi-gated and found to be rooted in two groups of factors. One con-cerns the inherent characteristics of the child and includes: "good intelligence, easy temperament, good interpersonal rela-tionships, a strong sense of self and a clear understanding of the parent's illness."[30] The other set of factors includes the presence of a strong social support system, both in and outside of the fami-ly.[31]

One of the most impressive examples of the preventive value of close supportive relationships has been reported by Brown and Harris, in England, who studied the impact of the loss of a parent in childhood on the subsequent development of depres-sion.[32] In a series of studies of inner-city women in London, they found that those women who lost a parent in childhood and had no other intimate relationships developed depression. Those who lost a parent in childhood but had good, supportive relation-ships, especially with the surviving parent, did not develop de-pression. These studies suggest "that the loss of care following the death of a parent was more important than the parental loss itself."[1]

Understanding of such protective mechanisms is obviously crucial to planning preventive strategies.[33]

SEVEN

Psychosocial Treatment

If you suspect that your child or someone under your care is significantly depressed for a period of at least several weeks, what can or should you do?

The first thing is to confirm your suspicion by consulting the child's pediatrician, your family physician, or the school nurse or counselor. These sources may either alleviate your worries by diagnosing the child's condition as a harmless, passing phase, or they may refer you to a child psychiatrist, psychologist, child guidance clinic, or community mental health center for further study. The more knowledge that one of these sources has about the child and the family, the more effectively and quickly administered treatment will be.

If professional help is recommended, two kinds of treatment should be sought. One is psychological treatment or psychotherapy, discussed in this chapter, and the other is pharmacological (drug) treatment, the topic of the next. The two are often used in combination.

Goals and Types of Psychotherapy

The all-encompassing goal of psychological therapy is to help the child reach the highest possible level of functioning, while alleviating mental pain or anguish. This goal may be reached through *insight, behavior modification,* or *counseling.* These general types, along with specific examples of their application, are described below.

The older established form of psychological therapy is based on psychodynamic principles, that is, on the premise that people's emotional difficulties arise from largely unconscious conflicts that lead to distorted views of themselves and others, frequently accompanied by painful feelings. This form of therapy, whether used with an individual, a family, or a group, has a common orientation: that is, to evoke insight into personal difficulties, provided the patient is intellectually and emotionally ready to accept it.

Perhaps more importantly, along with many other forms of therapy, psychodynamic therapy makes use of what British child analyst David Winnicott called the *holding situation,* which refers to stability and consistency in the therapist-patient environment.[1] Therapists employing this method of treatment use what psychiatrist Edward Strachey, in the 1930s, called the *mutative interpretation.* This technique encourages the patient to express bad things he feels about himself, which he then projects by attributing his bad characteristics to the therapist; if he's receiving therapy in a group, he may also project them onto some group members. The therapist and/or members of the group interpret to him his largely unconscious maneuver and by doing so give him back a corrected, realistic version of his often distorted ideas and feelings. If this process is sufficiently repeated, the patient may be encouraged to change and acquire a new idea or picture of himself and of the people in the world around him.

Another general method of psychological treatment is behavior modification. It is based on various learning and behavior theories that hold that human behavior is not governed by unconscious forces but, rather, shaped by specific environmental factors. Behaviorists stress environmental factors that influence behavior and pay little attention to insight or other intrapsychic factors. Their emphasis is on manipulating environmental conditions in order to alter specific target behaviors. Behavior alteration is often achieved by reward and punishment systems. So-called positive reinforcement involves a systems of rewards that may be tangible, such as food, money, or candy, or intangible, such as privileges or praise. Negative reinforcement seeks the extinction of undesirable behavior. The most common techniques employed toward this goal include purposefully ignoring an undesirable behavior or administering some form of punishment.

A variant of behavioral therapy is cognitive therapy, as developed by Aaron T. Beck[2] and modified for use in children by Maria Kovacs.[3] The basic assumption of this therapy is that emotional disturbances, including depression, are caused by distortions in thinking on a conscious level. According to this theory, the disturbed thinking of a depressed person includes three major elements: (1) negative self-esteem; (2) negative view of the past and present; and (3) hopeless outlook for the future. Cognitive therapy attempts to correct this disturbed thinking by direct logical examination and challenge of the patient's view of himself, his environment, and his destiny.

Interpersonal psychotherapy is a relatively recent but already very popular method of treatment. It focuses on depressive precipitants in the patient's life, such as interpersonal losses, role disputes and transitions, social isolation, or deficits in social skills. It advocates the acknowledgment and proper mourning of losses, encourages the improvement in social skills necessary to acquire social support, and promotes resolution of role conflicts. Interpersonal therapy seems especially useful in ameliorating the social aspects of the patient's dysfunction.[4]

The ultimate goal of any therapeutic intervention will vary from case to case, according to many factors. Some therapists and patients seek to relieve the present symptoms without attempting to alter the patient's basic personality characteristics. Others may be more ambitious and strive toward the realization of the patient's full potential. Such striving may be limited by the severity of the patient's past and present life circumstances and by the extent of the patient's motivation and determination to seek change. Sometimes even the most motivated patients and their families are frustrated and deterred by mundane circumstances, such as treatment availability and monetary and time considerations. Lack of health benefits can be a very real restriction to many needy individuals.

The child psychiatrist or other child therapist can choose from a number of types of treatment that usually are most useful in the earlier stages of the disorder. Many of those involve some kind of family intervention. This can include intensive family psychotherapy, in which all family members are encouraged to discuss what they know about the problem and the circumstances that precipitate it and are guided to see how changes in their own behavior may alleviate it. It can also include periodic counseling of the parents, with or without direct contact with the child.

Working with Families

All work with families calls for certain amounts of insight therapy and certain amounts of guidance, and children and parents may benefit from both. We've seen some patients for years and never given them advice. With other patients, almost the entire time of every therapy session is taken up with advice giving.

The choice of method will depend on the severity and length of the illness, the age of the child, and the intelligence, motivation, and insightfulness of the parents. The younger the child, the more responsive she or he will be to environmental changes alone. For example, a change in the amount of time that the mother or father is available to the child can be extremely helpful.

Parent Counseling

Mental health professionals sometimes see families who are not aware of the potential harm to the child of some of their child-rearing methods. For instance, one family that farmed out a child all week to a grandmother, bringing him home only for the weekend, was having problems. The mother, coming herself from an emotionally deprived background, had a lot of difficulty comprehending the traumatic effect of this arrangement. In this situation the therapist had to be directive in pointing out to the parents the relationship between the child's life situation and his depression. Explanations and interpretations of the child's feelings of rejection were not helpful or understood by this mother because of her own emotional limitations.

Other suggestions to the parent about the child may include: taking him during the weekends on outings, fishing, or picnics; taking her on shopping trips or to the library; helping him with his homework during the week. All activities will bring the parents closer to, or more in touch with, the child. Other suggestions may include helping the child cope more effectively with specific depressive issues that have arisen in the child's life. If there has been a recent death, the family will be advised to talk about it with the child openly and to answer frankly any questions he or she may have. Grief may be lightened by being brought out in the open. If the child is depressed about not having friends, the parents may be advised on how to teach and help the child make more friends—through such strategies as joining in a game at the playground, inviting children to a party or a cookout at home, or asking someone the child particularly likes to go to a movie as a guest.

Where the child is older, and of school age, or when depression is of long duration or great intensity, work with families should include the affected child and, often, other family members as well. In such cases, family therapy often has to be supplemented by individual work with the depressed child and with the parents—particularly if, as so often happens, one or both parents are depressed. Whenever it can be used, an interpretive (evocative) rather than directive form of therapy is most efficacious in producing long-term benefits. That's because it leads to insights about the family dynamics and how to balance the child's and the family's needs.

When the therapist tells the family to spend more time with the child or to stop sending him away during the week, he is using direct guidance. But when the therapist attempts to further the family's understanding of certain family dynamics in an effort to decrease depreciation and rejection of the child, he is using insight therapy. For example, scapegoating is a common practice in many families and leads to blaming the child for virtually every untoward event that occurs. Naturally, the child's self-esteem is negatively affected and low self-esteem is a cardinal mark of depression. With some families, the therapist can undo this process by helping parents understand that scapegoating makes a child feel worthless, inhibits his natural desire to accomplish things, and often makes him wonder if life is worth living. When family members come to realize this through insight, they are more likely to abandon the scapegoating pattern than if they are simply given direct advice such as: "Quit complaining about this child," or "Knock off blaming the child for things he did or didn't do." A person who reaches conclusions on his own is more likely to act firmly than a person who has been told what to do by someone else.

The same process of insight therapy can work when the child is depressed following a major loss. The therapy may explain that while children are able to substitute for lost love objects (see Chapter Two), they need help in finding such substitutes. Given these insights into the situation, many families can come to their own conclusions about what to do to correct it.

Another form of loss may involve marital discord or contemplated or completed divorce. It is essential to involve both divorced parents in this process rather than dealing with only the custodial parent.

A relatively recent development in modern society is the appearance of many single-parent families, as well as families where both parents are employed and out of the home a great deal. Such situations may represent a potential loss for the child, who misses spending time with his parents. If the child of overburdened, stressed parents becomes depressed, counseling for the child and parents is recommended.

Parent Therapy

If a parent has a depressive illness, it is very important to provide prompt appropriate treatment, in order to improve the parent's functioning and thus to furnish a nondepressed model for the child to follow and identify with.

Individual Therapy with the Child

The following reflects our predilection for an eclectic approach to psychiatric treatment rather than a narrow parochial view.

In some cases of childhood depression, family and parental treatment may not suffice and individual psychotherapy for the child may be indicated. The specific goals in such circumstances differ only somewhat from those set up for adult patients. The crucial one is the development of a close, empathic, and trusting relationship with the therapist. In addition to good professional qualifications, the therapist has to be an intuitive person sensitive to the child's needs. Many distinguished therapists, such as David Levy[5] and Frederick Allen,[6] have even gone so far as to say that such a close trusting relationship accounts for most successes achieved in psychotherapy with children. All would agree that it is the cornerstone of such therapeutic work.

Second in importance is what Franz Alexander calls a corrective emotional experience[7]: the child experiences a different and healthier response from his therapist than he had experienced earlier in his life. The therapist accepts the child in his totality without criticism or judgment. Where appropriate, he expresses approval of the child, which is often in contrast to the previously experienced constant disapproval. Since low self-esteem and hopelessness are the hallmarks of childhood depression, the therapist has to make special efforts to convey to the child that he values him as a person regardless of shortcomings and has firm hopes about the child's ability to overcome his difficulties and become a well-functioning, self-respecting person.

A third important element is encouraging the child to ventilate all negative feelings and thoughts—fears, worries, sadness, hopelessness, conflicts with important people, anger, and distortions of himself and others. Although Anna Freud stressed that such ventilation is not sufficient,[8] it is important that the child feel free to get things off his or her chest with appropriate affect in a nonthreatening and supportive situation.

As with adults and families, advice and counseling play important roles. Such devices may include encouraging the child to attempt new relationships or repair old ones that went awry because of misconceptions grown out of depressed feelings. Therapists and parents can also encourage children to get into things they are known to be good at. If they have been good at sports, they can be encouraged to become involved in athletic activities. If they have been good at or shown interest in musical activities, school dramatics, photography, dancing, the school newspaper, or any other activity, they can be encouraged to take it up. Participation in such work and play is a marvelous way of increasing the self-esteem and psychological strength of a depressed child.

The therapist may also discuss with the child a particular troubling situation and try to get the child to see what he or she can do to overcome it. For example, if lack of help with difficult homework is a cause of depressed feelings, the therapist can suggest how the child can go about asking a parent, brother, sister, or schoolmate for help with an especially tough assignment. Or, if the child is concerned about lack of playmates at home, the therapist may suggest asking the parent's permission to have friends over in exchange for doing chores around the house.

The final goal is helping the child to understand the basis of his or her feelings and conflicts. With the help of the therapist, the child has to learn to understand his or her unrealistic perceptions of himself or herself and others, his or her neurotic conflicts, and the alternative ways available to cope with life circumstances in a more effective and adaptive manner.

Sometimes all the above techniques fail because of the truly hopeless nature of the child's situation. It is crucial in such cases for the therapist to acknowledge such a reality and help the child to cope with it. The therapist may say: "It's clear that you can't do anything with your mother (father, sister, and so forth) that would help her to be more caring about you or like you more." Such statements indicate that a caring mutuality exists between the therapist and the child, which may represent the best hope for improvement in such a situation.

Although the goals of therapy are basically the same for all children, regardless of age, the technique employed obviously has to be tailored to the child's chronological age and cognitive or emotional readiness. In our experience, children as young as five or six can talk about their difficulties in a reasonable manner and require a minimum of nonverbal activities such as play or games to clarify their problems. But younger children require play therapy employing dolls and other play materials and games. Through play the child expresses in his or her own way all the problems older children verbalize more directly. The level of interpretation also has to be adjusted to the age and cognitive level of the child.

Most depressed children reared by caring parents or caretakers respond favorably to psychotherapy. One of the major factors responsible for this success is the maturational push children experience, which makes it easier for a child than an adult to change and mature (see Chapter Two).

Community Collaboration

There are many cases, of course, where family conditions make traditional psychiatric intervention infeasible. In such cases, the therapist may have to work with community resources, such as schools, juvenile courts, halfway houses, foster homes, and the police, on behalf of his depressed patients. In the course of treatment of depressed children, we have often gone to schools for meetings with the teachers, arranged for care in halfway houses or foster homes, talked to the police, and testified in court.

Hospitalization: A Way to Intervene in a Crisis Situation

For the vast majority of depressed children, hospitalization is *not* needed. In most instances, those who need hospitalization have a major depressive disorder, are acutely ill, frequently suicidal, and unable to function in their usual surroundings at home or school. In such cases, although hospitalization may at first seem frightening, it is most beneficial to the child. In an appropriate hospital situation—one with a department or ward specifically designed for seriously depressed youngsters—the children soon adjust to their new surroundings and often rapidly improve.

One of the most fascinating findings of our research to date has been the often relatively prompt and sustained improvement of many even chronically depressed children whom we admitted to hospital research wards. This was entirely unexpected, since we anticipated a temporary worsening of the depression as a result of separation from home and family. We believe that this phenomenon is due to the removal of the child from an often noxious environmental situation, coupled with the rallying of the family around the child who is labeled ill because of the hospitalization.

Obviously there are many hospitalized children from severely dysfunctional families who do not recover as rapidly and spontaneously as the children we have just described. For these children a more prolonged hospital stay may be necessary. Because of the increasing influence of managed medical care, hospitalizations for depression exceeding three to four weeks will rarely be approved and other forms of treatment must be used more effectively (e.g., day hospitals, residential treatment centers).

Psychopharmacological Treatment

O ur early understanding of the biological basis of depressive illness goes back to a chain of fortuitous events, antecedent to the general use of antidepressant drugs. It started with the introduction in the 1950s of antihypertensive drugs derived from the plant rauwolfia serpentina, long known and used in Indian folk medicine. The introduction of these drugs, marketed under the names Raudixin and Serpasil, was hailed at the time as a real breakthrough in the pharmacotherapy of hypertension. However, the clinical efficacy of these drugs was blemished by the fact that about 15 percent of the patients developed serious depression and some even committed suicide.[1-3] The cause of this strange phenomenon remained a mystery for a long time.

Later noted biochemist Bernard Brodie, at the National Institute of Mental Health, administered a rauwolfia-based drug to rodents and discovered that it dramatically lowered the brain content of both catecholamines and serotonin, producing a sedated state that has been described as an animal model of human depression.[4] This important discovery, coupled with the fact that all subsequently developed drugs that worked to lift depression raised the neurotransmitter levels in the central nervous system (CNS), led to the development of the biogenic amine theory of depression.[5-7]

The fact that Serpasil or Raudixin, when given in a reduced

dosage, were able to exert their antihypertensive action without inducing depression led some to speculate about a threshold phenomenon, wherein a certain minimal neurotransmitter level must be maintained to protect against the development of dysphoria or even depressive illness. Only 15 percent of the patients originally treated with Serpasil or Raudixin became depressed, which suggests the existence of a population subgroup with a vulnerability based on a lower basal level of one or several neurotransmitters. In this connection, it should be mentioned that the prevalence of serious affective disorders in the general population clusters in several epidemiological studies at the 10 to 15 percent level.

As this story reveals, medical discoveries are often serendipitous. So it has been with antidepressant drugs until recently. Some of the more important drugs are described below.

Imipramine

One of the most widely used drugs for depressive illness in adults and childhood depression is the tricyclic imipramine (Tofranil) and its derivatives. A Swiss doctor, Roland Kuhn,[8] accidentally discovered its value against depression in 1956 while looking for a drug that would be more effective against schizophrenia than one of the major tranquilizers, chlorpromazine. Imipramine turned out to be ineffective against schizophrenia but an excellent antidepressant.

Monoamine Oxidase (MAO) Inhibitors

The MAO inhibitors were derived from a compound, iproniazid, that had been developed in 1951 to combat the tubercle bacillus. It proved to be a powerful antituberculosis drug but also to have unexpected side effects, including euphoria and hyperactivity. This led some psychiatrists to try it as an antidepressant drug, which it proved to be.

The same year Kuhn was discovering the value of imipramine, Nathan Kline introduced iproniazid in America, treating depressed patients with good results.[9] Within a year, hundreds of thousands of patients all over the world were treated with this new medicine for depression.

Lithium

In its pure form, lithium is a very soft, whitish-gray metal. One of the basic elements, it was discovered early in the last century. Combined with carbonates, citrates, chlorides, and other such substances, it is known as a salt. In 1949, in fact, it was offered as a substitute for table salt (sodium chloride) in salt-restricted diets. The results were bad. Several patients afflicted with heart trouble died, and many with heart or kidney disease were poisoned. So the use of lithium virtually stopped.

Oddly, it was in that same year, 1949, that an obscure Australian physician, John Cade,[10] published a paper reporting a great discovery he had made about lithium—to which scarcely anyone paid any attention. Working in a crude laboratory in a small hospital, Cade was trying to test his idea that psychosis was caused by some toxic substance in the body. He injected urine from four groups of people—persons afflicted with mania, depression, or schizophrenia, and normal persons—into guinea pigs and noted the results. Some of the animals were not affected; the rest developed convulsions and died, whether the urine had come from sick or well people. The urine from some of the manic-depressives was especially powerful. Injected in quantities only one-third or one-fourth as large as samples from other persons, it paralyzed and killed the guinea pigs.

Now, what was the toxic agent? Cade eventually suspected uric acid and decided to administer it in pure form—combining it, however, with a solution of lithium salts. By doing so, he could more readily control its potency. He reran the experiment, this time supplementing the injections of urine with one of the uric acid and lithium combination. Surprisingly, all the injections proved to be far less toxic than the first time. Next, following an obvious trail, he injected lithium alone. It had a strong tranquilizing effect. The guinea pigs, when placed on their backs, instead of squealing and kicking as usual, just lay calmly. They were lethargic.

A simple association of ideas led Cade to try lithium on manic-depressive humans. It was the urine from such patients that had proved the most powerful in paralyzing and killing guinea pigs, and it was lithium that had calmed these restless animals. He used a group of subjects that included schizophrenics, depressives, and persons in the manic stage of manic-depression. He got the expected results: lithium had little or no effect on the people with schizophrenia or depression, but it produced tremendous improvement in those with mania. Cade wrote about one typical manic:

> This was a little wizened man of 51 who had been in a state of chronic manic excitement for five years. He was amiably restless, dirty, destructive, mischievous, and interfering. He had enjoyed a preeminent nuisance value in a back ward for all these years and bid fair to remain there for the rest of his life.
>
> The patient commenced treatment on March 29, 1948. On the fourth day the optimistic therapist thought he saw some change for the better but acknowledged that it could have been his expectant imagination; the nursing staff were noncommittal but loyal. However, by the fifth day it was clear that he was in fact more settled, tidier, less disinhibited and less distractable. From then on there was steady improvement so that in three weeks he was enjoying the unaccustomed and quite unexpected amenities of a convalescent ward.

After two months he was discharged and resumed a normal life at home. He took a small maintenance dose of lithium carbonate. Six months later, though, he was back in the hospital, as manic as ever. It turned out that he had felt so well that he had stopped taking his medicine. He went back on the lithium and became well again.

Cade's report was virtually ignored for some years, particularly in the United States, where lithium was a bad word because, as recounted earlier, it had one been used as a salt substitute and had killed several people who had heart disease. In Europe, however, a spirited campaign in favor of lithium's use was begun in the mid-1950s by a noted professor of biological psychiatry at Aarhus University, Denmark—Mogens Schou.[11] He had discovered Cade's reports, tried lithium himself on manic-depressives, found that it was indeed efficacious, and began enthusiastically to spread the good news. Ronald R. Fieve and Ralph Wharton at the New York State Psychiatric Institute introduced lithium treatment in America.

Although the older antidepressants and other psychiatric medications were discovered by chance, they served several very important functions: (1) They represented the first effective treatment in a field which hitherto had none. (2) They helped to focus the mental health profession on the medical aspects of psychiatric illness, including depression. This eventually brought psychiatry closer to other medical specialties, after decades of isolation. (3) They made crucial contributions to our understanding of a biological basis of depressive illness and to the initial development of rational pharmacotherapy of this disorder, which has proceeded apace over the last ten to fifteen years.[12,13]

As one investigator noted, "The change from a process dependent on chance to one based on rational design involves selecting a target of interest, such as uptake pump or receptor, and then developing a drug to affect that target, while at the same time avoiding effects on other potential targets," thus minimizing side effects.[12]

Use of Drugs in Adult Treatment

The number of antidepressant drugs has dramatically increased in the last several years, with the addition of several new compounds. The drugs now include:

1. Cyclic antidepressants, including the now venerable tricyclic antidepressants (TCAs), for a long time the main staple of antidepressant treatment; the related tetracyclic drugs, such

as amoxapine (Asendin) and maprotiline (Ludiomil); and the newer heterocyclic drugs buproprion (Wellbutrin) and trazodone (Desyrel).

2. Monoamine oxidase inhibitors (MAOIs).
3. Selective serotonin reuptake inhibiting drugs (SSRIs), which include the well publicized fluoxetine (Prozac), sertraline (Zoloft), paroxetine (Paxil), and several other contenders to be added shortly.
4. Lithium.

The newer cyclic antidepressants, as well as the SSRIs, differ from the classic drugs in structure, as well as in their biological functions and side effect profiles. They are quite useful in patients who do not respond to the traditional drugs or cannot tolerate their side effects. As a group, the newer compounds are less dangerous if an overdose occurs.

The expansion of the class of drugs labeled antidepressants presents the clinician with new opportunities and challenges. Patients who were previously unresponsive to or intolerant of drugs (because of intolerable side effects) can be now offered useful, often lifesaving alternatives. On the other hand, because each of the new compounds follows a different metabolic path, it behooves the prescribing physician to familiarize himself/herself with the fundamentals of the biological actions of these drugs. This will allow for a more rational choice among the available medications. Studies are underway, the results of which will allow clinicians to match patients with specific symptom profiles with the right medications, without having to wait three to four or more weeks for clinical improvement or lack of it (the latter forcing a change of antidepressant medication, with another potential delay of several weeks).

Studies indicate[14] that patients who exhibit a satisfactory response to an antidepressant agent for a first episode of depression should continue to receive a full therapeutic dose of the drug for at least sixteen to twenty weeks after achieving full remission. During the first eight weeks after symptom resolution the person is particularly vulnerable to relapse.

Many patients who experience a first episode of major depression are likely to have a recurrence, usually within two or three years. Patients who are prone to recurrences should be considered candidates for continuous prophylactic drug treatment during remissions, especially if any of the depressive episodes was complicated by serious suicidal ideation or attempts, psychotic features, or severe functional impairments. There is as yet no definitive information on the appropriate duration of such maintenance therapy. Some studies suggest a five-year period.[15] However, for some patients with frequent depressive episodes, maintenance treatment may be required indefinitely.

In the past, simultaneous treatment with several antidepressant drugs was generally discouraged. However, recently such an approach has been described as effective in many cases where the depression does not respond adequately to a single antidepressant drug.[16]

In addition to their use in mood disorders, antidepressant drugs are often effective in many other psychiatric conditions. Some of these include: anxiety disorders, such as phobias, panic and obsessive-compulsive disorders; hyperactivity, aggressive and other impulse disorders; post-traumatic stress and some personality disorders. The common thread uniting these diverse clinical entities is the presence of a dysphoric mood (sadness, anger, and anxiety).

Drug Treatment of Bipolar Disorder

Lithium is most useful in the treatment of bipolar illness, though it is often used in cases of major depression as well. This dual role for lithium is based on the fact that the two types of mood disorder have similar biological mechanisms and share a common hereditary basis, although their manifestations are different.

The introduction of the anticonvulsant drugs carbamazepine (Tegretol) and valproic acid (Depakene) was a major innovation in the treatment of bipolar illness that did not respond to lithium. These drugs are sometimes useful in the management of antidepressant drug-resistant unipolar depression.

It is generally recommended that the drug treatment of bipolar disorders be continued for several years and, for some patients, indefinitely.[17]

Increasing public recognition of the ubiquity of mood disorders has helped to transform the previously encountered reluctance to take medication into acceptance of depression as a legitimate illness that may require drug treatment—much like, say, cardiovascular illness. The downside of this near universal acceptance of antidepressant medication is the fact that it often fosters their use in situations where no serious psychiatric disorder exists and distorts the therapeutic focus when the complaint is a vague personality problem, such as shyness, social uneasiness, emotional hypersensitivity, low frustration tolerance—to mention just a few. Use of antidepressant drugs with such personality traits has been designated "cosmetic psychopharmacology" by Peter Kramer in *Listening to Prozac*.[18] It has become especially frequent since the introduction of the SSRIs, which have been widely prescribed. Kramer's book captured the public imagination and led to many cover stories in national magazines on Prozac. Since these drugs have not been rigorously tested in controlled studies for disorders other than major depression, one has to guard against the notion that any antidepressant drug represents a universal "happy pill." Unwarranted use of these drugs is not without hazards, causing annoying or even serious side effects in many patients.

By the way, Hagop Akiskal, Director of the International Mood Center of the University of California, San Diego, believes that the SSRIs do not alter the basic personality; rather "among dysthymics there is a depressive inertia. If you remove it, the smoothly functioning personality of that individual emerges."[19]

The cyclic drugs and SSRIs are believed to block the reuptake of norepinephrine or serotonin into the nerve cells that released it, where it would be deactivated or destroyed. The MAO inhibitors work by blocking the action of the enzyme whose job is to break down the neurotransmitters. Thus, all of these drugs work, albeit in different ways, to keep more of the neurotransmitters active in the synapses or spaces between nerve cells.

The exact action of lithium in affective disorders has not yet been fully clarified. However, two theories have been proposed. One emphasizes the action of lithium on the movement of two electrolytes, sodium and potassium, in and out of the nerve cell. The second theory suggests that lithium eliminates the surplus of neurotransmitters at the synapse, believed to underlie manic disorders. However, this latter theory does not explain lithium's effectiveness in the treatment of some unipolar depressions.

Electroshock treatment is often used with affectively disordered adults who are acutely ill but do not respond quickly enough to drugs. It is usually successful, though no one knows exactly the mechanism involved. There is some evidence that it also affects the action of neurotransmitters. Its use in children is extremely rare.

Treating Children with Drugs

Since the 1960s, we have witnessed a rapid increase in the use of psychoactive drugs with children and adolescents. This has been caused by greater diagnostic clarity, better understanding of pediatric pharmacokinetics, and refinement of research methodology. Another potent factor is the idea that similarities in the clinical features of childhood and adult disorders may suggest a similar biological dynamic and drug response.

During the last decade, in particular, children have been more frequently prescribed antidepressant drugs, particularly the tricyclic antidepressants, such as imipramine (Tofranil), desipramine (Norpramin), amitriptyline (Elavil), and nortriptyline (Pamelor). It has been reported that these medications can ameliorate or reverse a great variety of psychopathological diagnostic entities, such as attention deficit hyperactivity disorder, conduct disorder, separation anxiety, school phobia, obsessive compulsive disorder, enuresis, and, of course, depression. Of all these disorders one would expect depression to be the most responsive, since many studies[20-22] indicate that children and adolescents suffer from similar and possibly identical depressive syndromes as adults. As a result, many psychiatrists, pediatricians, and family practitioners use antidepressant drugs in the treatment of depressed children and adolescents.

Although antidepressant drugs were used in children as early as the 1960s, the reports of that era were not rigorous and included children with heterogenous and poorly delineated disorders, as well as arbitrary dosages and treatment schedules. It was only in the 1970s that diagnostic criteria, interview schedules, and depression rating scales for children and adolescents were standardized, which allowed for more rigorous studies of the efficacy of antidepressant drugs in this age group.

This has resulted in several reviews of properly conducted studies of antidepressants in children.[23,24] Surprisingly, these reviews do not confirm the effectiveness of antidepressant drugs in ameliorating depression in either children or adolescents. In fact, no published modern study has provided evidence of the superiority of these drugs over placebo. In some studies, antidepressants actually appear to be *less* effective than placebos. The results of these studies are in stark contrast to the confirmed—and growing—trend among clinicians to use antidepressants in children.

These perplexing findings prompted the National Institute of Mental Health (NIMH) to convene a meeting of leading investigators in the field in July 1990, in a attempt to assess the current state of our knowledge and to clarify the problems involved.[25] While the emphasis was on the treatment of adolescent depression, the deliberations were relevant to childhood depression as well.

Many hypotheses were proposed to explain the meager response to antidepressant drugs seen in the studies. It was suggested[26] that childhood depression may represent a more severe form of depression than that which begins in adulthood, akin to juvenile diabetes or juvenile rheumatoid arthritis, both of which show worse prognosis and less response to treatment than their adult counterparts. However, many other less ominous explanations have been proposed. The simplest one points out that approximately 25 percent of children diagnosed as depressed recover spontaneously within two weeks. Obviously, any treatment administered during this period, drug or placebo, may result in artificially inflated rates of clinical improvement. Another hypothesis is that, while bipolar illness is relatively rare in childhood, the onset of depression in childhood foretells the development of a bipolar disorder, which would respond to lithium rather than to cyclic antidepressant drugs.[27]

Some investigators link the lack of response to antidepressant drug treatment in studies of depressed children and adolescents to the relatively short duration of treatment in many of these studies. Perhaps many short-term drug trials have disappointing results because treatment effects take longer to develop in depressed youngsters. A trial of at least ten to twelve weeks might improve the rate of recovery.

Other investigators stress the biological developmental changes from childhood to adulthood, which may affect the clinical expression of depression. Studies in rhesus monkeys indicate that noradrenergic activity increases and reaches a peak the end of adolescence, while monoamine oxidase activity decreases. Serotonergic receptors in rat brain may be decreased after adolescence, and there is evidence that cholinergic activity in animals and humans increases until puberty and then declines. Thus, developmental neurotransmitter changes, which are still poorly understood, may be responsible for the disparity in response to antidepressant drugs in various age groups.[25]

We are reminded by this controversy of the early reviews of adult drug treatment in the 1970s, when it was reported that at least a third of the then available studies indicated that antidepressant drugs in adults showed no greater efficacy than placebo. Since then, more sophisticated studies have clearly demonstrated the clinical efficacy of antidepressant drugs in adults. One has to keep in mind that only a few rigorous studies have been done in children and adolescents, with the total number of patients not exceeding two hundred fifty to three hundred subjects.

As mentioned earlier, the preponderance of childhood studies utilized the tricyclic antidepressants and only a few involved alternative drugs, which have been found to be very effective with adults, such as monoamine oxidase inhibitors, heterocyclic drugs, tricyclics combined with lithium, and the newer serotonergic drugs.

It is interesting that the negative findings mentioned above have not deterred clinicians from widely using tricyclic antidepressants in children. Even many of the investigators who reported negative findings in their own studies have continued to use these drugs in their clinical practice.

There may be several explanations for this apparent paradox. To begin with, unlike researchers, many clinicians do not exclude children who do not fulfill the strict *DSM-IV* criteria for major depression; instead, they are guided by such factors as mood instability, vegetative symptoms, suicidality, aggressivity, severity of depression, and a strongly positive family history of depression. The possibility exists that, by insisting on the use of strict *DSM-IV* criteria, investigators exclude many potential responders to antidepressant medication. Clinicians may use a wider net and monitor their patients with a broader range of observations than are followed in research studies. Although the rating scales used in research protocols may be more systematic than clinicians' assessment, they may leave out important information needed for monitoring drug response.[28]

Nevertheless, these reports raise numerous questions for clinicians. Are the many positive responses to antidepressants that physicians, parents, teachers, and children themselves report due largely to nonbiological mechanisms? What should a clinician tell parents and patients when recommending a medicine that published reports suggest is ineffective? Such issues become even more cogent with ongoing concern about the possibility that antidepressant use may be associated with sudden death in some younger children.[29] Can one justify their use? On the other hand, should the small number of studies, each with its own methodological weaknesses, override the widespread belief of clinicians in the value of using antidepressant drugs in this age group? Obviously, the answer will come only from more research studies, using more sophisticated and diverse types of inquiries.

Many physicians feel that the tricyclic drugs, when given in high doses, as they often have to be in children, may adversely affect the child's heart function.[30] Although the tricyclics do work well in adults and are probably safe with careful monitoring of heart function, the newer drugs, especially the SSRIs, may turn out to be a safer alternative for children.[22]

In recent years, lithium has been increasingly used in the treatment of children. Children reportedly responsive to lithium include those who are hyperactive, undergo cyclic mood changes, exhibit aggressive behavior, and have explosive outbursts. Eventually it may be found that all of these conditions are early manifestations of bipolar disorders,[31] in which lithium proves particularly effective. Our own studies indicate that children with bipolar disorders respond well to lithium.[32] We'd like to report about two of our cases.

Marilyn was eight when she was brought to us on an emergency basis by her mother, a professor at nearby university. She had always been moody, her mother said, had had a number of serious depressive episodes, and had gone through several high periods, when she didn't sleep well at night and was overbusy and overexuberant. Because the mother had a bipolar illness herself and had done well on lithium, she suspected that her daughter might be developing a manic-depressive disorder. The situation became critical when Marilyn made a suicide attempt.

When her mother brought Marilyn to us, the girl was markedly depressed. We involved her in a research program we had started in order to learn what types of children responded to lithium. We were giving children lithium for four weeks followed by placebo for four weeks, then taking them off all pills, and finally, giving them lithium again. We would repeat this procedure several times in order to make sure that the children who responded were indeed responding to lithium and not just to the fact that they were in the program or were hearing things from us that may have been unintentionally therapeutic.

Every time Marilyn got lithium she responded to it; she became noticeably and definitely less depressed. And every time the placebo was substituted for lithium she became very depressed again. After the research program was completed, we put her on lithium on a regular basis. That was about sixteen years ago. Ever since, except for two episodes when she stopped the lithium on her own—as most patients do because they think they don't need it anymore—Marilyn has remained on lithium. The times she stopped taking it, she became quite depressed and had to come see us again and get started on her medication. She has done extremely well and is now a most personable and well-adjusted young woman.

The other patient we'd like to mention is Dora, an eleven-year-old girl who had been having mood swings—more pronounced than Marilyn's—for about a year. During a manic period she would stay up most of the night, writing letters to her friends and reading books; during the day she would participate in every school activity she could possibly find. She was a cheerleader, tried out for one athletic team after another, worked on the school newspaper—was in fact so overactive that the school staff became distressed. This was the closest to a true manic state that we have seen in a child. Alternating with these highs, she had serious lows, during which she became very depressed, withdrawn, and attempted to harm herself.

Dora, like Marilyn, was put into our lithium research program and responded well. She has been maintained on lithium for some years and is now functioning at a very high level and is grateful for having been treated. Like Marilyn, she stopped her medicine several times because she felt she no longer needed it. Each time, she relapsed and became depressed, she returned to see us, was put back on lithium, and soon was doing well again.

Most children who respond to lithium get clearly better in four to seven days. In contrast to experience with adults, our studies confirm earlier reports that side effects in children are relatively rare. However, neither the ultimate safety of lithium in children nor the size of the maintenance dose necessary to prevent relapses has been definitely determined. It would seem prudent to avoid using lithium where the patient has kidney, cardiovascular, or thyroid disease, to periodically screen the thyroid and kidney function, and to use caution in determining how long to use the medicine.

Drugs or Psychotherapy?

The best treatment currently offered for affective disorders combines psychotherapy and psychopharmacology. Such combination is more efficacious than using either method alone, especially in the major (both unipolar and bipolar) types of the disorder.[33-36] This applies to adults as well as children. There are several reasons why merely giving someone lithium or an antidepressant drug without some form of psychotherapy or counseling is considered second-rate treatment.

Because of their often long-standing depressive disorder, many patients have not learned how to effectively cope with their day-to-day problems. They often have deficiencies in their abilities to relate to other people and to handle their emotions. Some have lived with this situation for many years. Even people with a situational depression caused by a reaction to adverse life circumstances may have a distorted view of other people and the world, having used inefficient psychological defenses before seeking help. Antidepressant drugs can correct or at least put into better order the chemical imbalance in their brain, but it does not undo all the years of suffering caused by being overwhelmed by their troubled emotions, having a distorted view of reality and a pervasive sense of hopelessness and despair. The latter issues can only be solved or ameliorated through psychotherapy, which may restore the emotional balance as well.

The American Psychiatric Association has published guidelines to treatment of unipolar[37] and bipolar[38] affective disorders in adults. This important step may lead to more focused, rational, and standardized pharmacological and psychosocial treatment of children as well. In addition, current and future treatment outcome studies should bring some order to a field where unproven, "anything goes" treatment methods still abound.

Guidelines to Handling Depressed Children

Seldom do we look upon children as small human beings, struggling like the rest of us to make sense of life, to satisfy needs, and to meet challenges as they arise. We tend to assume that children are somehow protected by their innocence. Nevertheless, one way children differ from adults is in the overwhelming number of new experiences with which they must cope. Meeting for the first time the child next door, entering the wonderful and bewildering world of the supermarket, going on an airplane trip, starting nursery school or kindergarten, changing living places—all these and hundreds of other adventures may be scary or pleasant or stressful, depending mainly on the child's temperament, but also to some extent on the way that parents or other close figures have prepared her to meet such experiences.

The complexity of human behavior, difficult for adults to unravel in the best of circumstances, is more so for children. In the process of realizing their potential and learning to deal with newness, they are developing—and *changing as they develop*. Lois Murphy describes this process of change as follows:[1]

> During the first four or five years of life most children are confronted with demands to accept and come to terms with numerous new situations. Some of these involve challenges to engage in new activities which may require the integra-

tion of new coordinations and skills, however well established some of the elements of these may be. Some of the skills demanded are not merely new, but difficult for the child's level of development, maturity and capacity. New challenges may accordingly arouse some apprehension. The effort to deal with both internal tensions and external pressures optimally evokes spontaneous, constructive efforts which are however realistically limited by the child's total resources at that point. These coping efforts are enhanced in certain children, and in other children constrained or decreased by the tension aroused by the possibility of failure.

Many parents speak of *stages* that children go through, usually meaning periods of irritating or difficult behavior. Sometimes they're right: a difficult or faddish period may indeed be a stage from which the child will safely emerge. But sometimes these parents are wrong, and they are never more wrong than when they think of a serious childhood depression as a stage or a temporary condition.

Parents may make this mistake because they have noticed that the child is continually changing; they reason that her depressive behavior may change, and it often does. Or they may feel that just as children outgrow thumb sucking, bedwetting, fear of the dark, and lying, particularly if they have understanding and loving parents, they will probably outgrow their depressive mood or behavior. But parents commonly fail to recognize a serious childhood depression as something for which both they and the child may need help. The child herself usually recognizes that something is wrong, and she is generally the best source of information for the person called upon to make a diagnosis. In acting-out behavior, the reverse is true—parents are much more likely than the child to report disturbing symptoms and situations.

Learning to Listen to and Talk with Your Child

Depressive and other disturbed behaviors do not always simply fade away. They hang on and cause recurrent difficulties. Most often the child knows that he or she is in trouble but doesn't talk about it. You, the parent, must start the talking—and listen well to what the child tells you. When you suspect that something is wrong with your son or daughter—when the child is not engaging in his or her usual activities, when he or she isn't having fun with his friends, when he or she is moping around the house, when he or she is falling behind in his schoolwork—you should say something like: "Is something bothering you? Have you been feeling bad? Are you upset?" Children aged six to twelve (latency-age children) and even some younger children more likely will tell you about it. They'll tell you how sad they are, that they've been crying, that they don't have any friends, that they're not doing well at school, that they feel bad about their whole lives. What they tell you is often not easy to listen to, and it may become difficult to ask about. You must do the asking, though, for the sake of your child's emotional health. Choose a quiet time and place—after a meal, perhaps, and in the child's favorite room—and quietly fire away.

Normal Depression

Transient depressive reactions are very common among children, as they are among adults. Every child will display occasional periods of sadness, loneliness, self-depreciation, tearfulness, loss of interest in his or her usual activities, and disturbances of appetite or sleep.

These short-lived episodes usually follow a specific traumatic event. Janie, for instance, had lost her favorite doll, and no amount of searching had turned it up. Robert had quarreled with his best friend. Brenda's father had promised to take her to the amusement park, but at the last minute had been called in due to emergency at work. The transitory depressions that follow such events generally last no longer than a few days, a week or two at most, except for bereavement following the loss of a loved one, such as a parent, sibling, friend, or even a favorite pet. In such cases, symptoms of depression lasting as long as six months are considered part of a normal grief reaction. Parents should do what any normal human being does for someone who is suffering: be sympathetic and caring. But there is no need for clinical help.

Likewise, moving, with the concomitant loss of friends, neighborhood, school, and home, often sets off a mild depression that frequently lasts until the child begins to feel at home in the new environment.

So, under many circumstances, a depressive response is normal. But when the response or reaction becomes more intense, lasts longer, and, in particular, is not related to an obvious source of stress, it is time to be concerned, for a mental illness may be in the making. This is especially true if functioning with friends, family, and at school is impaired.

Recognizing a Depressive Illness

The exact line between a normal depression and a depression that is or may become a mental illness can be difficult to draw. But there are a number of signs and symptoms that should alert parents, teachers, and doctors to the presence of a more serious disorder if they last too long or are of at least moderate intensity.

Of all the possible danger signs, the two most important by far are these:

1. *Dysphoric mood* (the word is from the Greek for "poor attitude"). The child feels sad, blue, hopeless, low, down in the dumps, worried, and irritable.
2. *Anhedonia* (without pleasure). The child lacks interest or doesn't take pleasure in most usual activities, such as sports, hobbies, or interactions with friends, or family.

Other signs are:

- Poor appetite and weight loss or, on the contrary, excessive eating.
- Sleep disturbances, such as insomnia, sleeplessness, nightmares, restless sleep, and early morning awakening. Excessive sleep may be an indicator, too.
- A loss of energy that shows itself in lying around the house and feeling tired, listless, fatigued.
- Psychomotor agitation, which is apparent when the child is restless, fidgety, unable to sit still.
- Self-reproach or excessive or inappropriate guilt. The child has a tendency to blame herself for everything that goes wrong in her environment. For example, she may show guilt over school grades even though her performance has been better than average, or guilt over parental quarrels even though she had nothing to do with them.
- Diminished ability to think and concentrate. This may be observed in ordinary conversation but is more frequently seen in a drop in school performance.
- Recurrent thoughts of death or suicide, or any suicidal behavior. Such thoughts may be brought up spontaneously by the child or may be elicited gently during conversation.

Seeking Professional Help

If you suspect a depressive problem in a child, what is the best course to follow? In the beginning, we would counsel waiting. Reactive depressions, including grief reactions, are not only common but self-limiting; that is, they often improve without intervention. Also, it's worth talking with and listening to the child, to probe deeper into her world, depressive or not. However, if the symptoms noted above persist or worsen, help should be sought.

This help may be a visit to a pediatrician or a consultation with your priest, minister, rabbi, or school counselor. Having seen many children, these professionals usually can clarify and evaluate matters. They are in a good position to help you decide whether further help is needed; a consultation with a psychiatrist or another mental health professional with special expertise in treating children may be particularly helpful.

How to Help at Home

While professional help is important, there are also important measures parents can take. First, avoid scapegoating when dealing with the child. Scapegoating is the tendency to single out a child and blame him for anything that goes wrong in the family's life, whether or not he is at fault. This process can be very subtle and sometimes takes utmost diligence to detect. The problem is complicated by the depressed child's tendency to accept blame.

Next, give a depressed child special amounts of attention, praise, and emotional support. The most important kind of emotional support is the personal involvement of the parents with the child. Generally speaking, the depressed child needs extra time with the parents alone. Often, other relatives—brothers, sisters, grandparents, uncles, and aunts—can be brought into the picture. Depending on circumstances, warm involvement with other relatives can be the best form of treatment.

Finally, when losses occur, allow the child the freedom to work through her grief. In other words, allow her to end the grief by grieving. When the grieving process is ended prematurely, there may well be a depressive illness later in life. Once the grief has run its course, give the child every assistance in finding substitute persons and things to love.

Children who feel sad, blue, low, down in the dumps, or hopeless often don't reveal their feelings to their parent. They may show them to their friends, or they may keep them to themselves. You almost always have to ask the child how he or she is feeling. There is a notable exception—irritability. When a child is feeling sad and blue, she will often display irritability, and a parent can usually pick this up. When you find your normally pleasant child irritated with friends or by schoolwork or by every little vicissitude in life, it's time to ask if anything is bothering him or her. Ask specifically: "Have you been feeling sad or blue?" The answer will often be "yes," and you'll have started the ball rolling.

Watchful parents should be able to pick up just as readily the feelings of the child who has lost pleasure in everything. Take, for example, the child whose favorite hobby is building model airplanes. Suddenly you notice that the models are just sitting around. You begin paying attention to his other activities and notice that the train set is not being played with, that the bicycle is not being ridden, and that the child is no longer having friends in or going out to meet them.

Poor appetite, another sign of depression, should be very evident. The depressed child will say he doesn't want anymore, and all the pushing in the world won't get you very far.

Children won't generally tell you about sleep disturbances without being asked. But you'll notice that they're quite tired even though they seem to have been sleeping enough. Or you will hear them up early in the morning and wonder why.

A loss of energy is very clear. You'll notice the child lying around the house, with no get-up-and-go. Psychomotor agitation is rather rare in depressed children, but it is easy to spot when it occurs. The child may be fidgety and all over the place and you may feel you are being driven out of your mind. This is especially true when depression and attention deficit hyperactivity disorder coexist.

When irritability occurs, there is often self-reproach. Not only will the child complain about school and just about everything else in his life, but he will also go on to say that it's all his fault. He feels terrible. "Why are my grades falling off? Because I'm so stupid." "Why did I have to miss that goal in soccer game? I just wasn't giving it enough attention." "Why can't I ride my bike better? It's all my fault because I don't try hard enough." Depressed kids are down on themselves for everything.

Difficulty with thinking and concentrating, another mark of depression, is usually very hard for a parent to detect and is more likely to be picked up by a schoolteacher.

Thoughts about suicide and death are almost never mentioned spontaneously by children. But if you're worried about sadness, irritability, or self-reproach in a child, it's important to ask him or her about such thoughts. Half of the children we've studied have admitted to suicidal thoughts.

In closing this chapter, we should like to emphasize that the grieving child doesn't usually show grief the way adults do. What you will see in the grieving child is not so much irritability or self-reproach as a tendency toward not enjoying usual activities. One of the best things to do with such children is to give them an opportunity and encourage them to ventilate their feelings. Depending on the situation, say to them: "Gee, you miss Grandma as much as I do," or "Haven't you missed Timmy since he was hit by that automobile?" or "Isn't it sad that poor old Shep died?" Often they will talk very openly about the loss—often crying and displaying appropriate feelings. But, as noted earlier, you have to elicit this information from the child. Otherwise he will mope around quietly, and you will just think about your own sadness (if the loss was yours as well as his) and never know that your child is quite as sad as you are.

Prevention

Depression is a major health hazard, wreaking havoc on mental and physical functioning, contributing heavily to family dysfunction, and causing enormous financial losses, both in cost of treatment and in loss of productivity and income. Can we envision preventive public health measures, akin to mass immunizations against infectious diseases, for depression? Such "emotional immunization" would require development of effective defenses against a "pathogen," that is, the environmental factors contributing to the development or continuation of affective illness. Some of these defenses have been discussed in other parts of this book. Of particular importance is the strengthening of the parent-child bond, development of social skills, assertiveness training, massive and timely intervention in natural disasters, and provision of wide social resources for those at risk. Here we look at some broader societal measures and innovative programs.

Educating the Public

A preventive approach to affective disorders can succeed only in an educated, enlightened community. And that can develop only when age-old prejudices and superstitions about mental disorders are swept away.

The public needs to know that affective disorder is an illness and not a curse or visitation. As with many other illnesses, its causes can be studied; effective treatment is available for the majority of those afflicted by it, and amelioration for the rest. People with affective disorders have inalienable rights, including those to the best treatment available and to complete equality in their private, public, and professional lives. Only when such basic values are clarified and accepted will society begin to take preventive measures seriously.[1]

Fortunately, there are several promising developments afoot. In the best American tradition of self-help, several organizations formed and governed by former patients and their families in alliance with mental health professionals have launched a formidable effort to educate the public. Foremost among them are the National Alliance for the Mentally Ill and the National Depression and Manic-Depression Association.

The major professional organizations in general psychiatry, child and adolescent psychiatry, psychology, and social work are committed to raising public awareness of the ubiquity and endemic nature of affective disorders and of the measures needed to combat this "bane of human spirit."[2] The success of the annual "National Depression Screening Day" illustrates the power of these initiatives.

Meanwhile, many courageous, well-known, and respected public figures have "gone public," disclosing their own painful experiences with unipolar and bipolar affective disorders. Among them are writers, artists, television and movie personalities, politicians, journalists, athletes, and mental health professionals. The list is long and includes such luminaries as William Styron, Art Buchwald, Patty Duke, Mike Wallace, and Dr. Kay Jamison, one of the foremost researchers of bipolar disorders. Their courage has increased awareness of and improved attitudes toward mental illness in general and depressive and manic-depressive disorders in particular.

Several efforts now underway will enrich our meager database on prevention of mental illness. For instance, the American Academy of Child Psychiatry mounted a massive intervention initiative called "Project Prevention," which culminated in a landmark publication, *Prevention of Mental Disorders, Alcohol and Other Drug Use in Children and Adolescents*. This work serves to educate child and adolescent psychiatrists and other mental health professionals about the many identifiable risk factors that can be modified through early preventive interventions.[3]

In another arena, the appropriations committee of the U.S. Senate recognized that a strategic approach to the prevention of mental disorders is urgently needed. To this end "the Congress mandated the National Institute of Mental Health to enter into an agreement with the Institute of Medicine to review the current status on the prevention of mental illness . . . and provide recommendations on future research and implementation" in this vital area. This undertaking brought together an impressive array of leading mental health experts, whose deliberations were summarized in *Reducing Risks for Mental Disorders*.[4]

In 1990, the U.S. Senate and House of Representatives charged the National Institute of Mental Health with providing a blueprint to encourage more research into child and adolescent mental disorders—the so-called "National Plan." In February 1995, the American Academy of Child Psychiatry made public an interim assessment of this ongoing program, entitled *Report Card on the National Plan for Research on Child and Adolescent Mental Disorders*.[5] The report indicated that funding for clinical research on prevention of mental disorders in children and adolescents almost doubled between 1987 and 1994. However, the goal of reducing the prevalence of such disorders was not met. Dr. James Leckman of Yale University, who chaired the committee that issued the report, stated that "26 percent of Americans are under eighteen years of age and 7.5 million children and adolescents living in the United States suffer from mental disorders, often for life." The report further emphasized that more than 20 percent of American children live in poverty, and that risks to the mental health of the young, such as child abuse, urban violence, school dropout, and teenage pregnancy, are on the rise.

Counseling Those at Risk

A cohesive, economically and emotionally secure family provides the best soil for the child's emotional growth and good mental health. Stabilizing the family unit in disadvantaged areas requires bold new approaches, departing from the traditional ones in psychiatry, psychology, and social work, which have not proven effective. The major task is to help overcome the hopelessness, inertia, and fatalistic attitudes that hinder implementation of preventive measures.

Two child psychiatrists have distinguished themselves through their pioneering work on prevention of mental illness, with emphasis on parental involvement. James Comer from Yale University created a highly successful program coordinating a mental health team, a school management team, and a program to encourage and involve parents.[6] The other psychiatrist, William Beardsley from Harvard, developed a cognitive-psychoeducational intervention for use in families where one parent had a depressive disorder. This program helped children become aware of the stressors associated with parental depression and taught them coping strategies based on self-understanding and social relationships.[7,8]

Some stresses on children relate to our changing social scene. The rate of divorce in modern societies is high; in fact, in the United States one of every two marriages is likely to end in divorce. It is estimated that about one million children are added each year to the ranks of the offspring of divorced parents in this country. Wallerstein[9] has shown that children of divorced parents are at increased risk for a variety of depressive, behavioral, and anxiety disorders. In addition, she has pointed out two factors that may prevent or at least ameliorate such malignant outcome: (1) Both divorced parties share responsibility for the children's upbringing and remain intimately involved in their daily life, rather than being distant and detached, and (2) both divorced parents, in spite of their frequent resentment and animosities, strive to maintain an open line of civilized communication and cooperation regarding all aspects of their children's lives.

Divorced parents must be guided by the welfare of their children, rather than by their anger and resentment toward each other. While many divorcing parents could benefit from counseling, thereby minimizing the emotional hazards to their children, relatively few seek such guidance and help. Fortunately, several states and counties have instituted laws requiring counseling for couples contemplating divorce, as well as for their children. Such laws, if universally enacted, may help to reduce the risk of mental distress in a whole segment of our population.[10] These children will also benefit from programs developed specifically to meet their needs.[11]

Loss of a parent may be a forerunner of a mood disorder. Such an outcome may be mitigated by a universal recognition and acceptance of the value of grief counseling for children who experience trauma—not only death of a parent but also catastrophic events such as hurricanes, terrorist acts, or war. The long-term psychic damage of such events is well documented. For instance, a recent report from war-torn Bosnia indicates a striking prevalence of depressive symptomatology and suicidal ideation among the children there.[12] The value of counseling in such traumatic situations is also well recognized, as attested by the mobilization of hundreds of mental health professionals to counsel the survivors of the bombing in Oklahoma City on April 19, 1995. Since natural and man-made disasters are unavoidable, thought should be given to having such disaster counseling teams or networks kept in readiness, akin to "emotional fire fighting."

Genetic Counseling

In 1993, a workshop sponsored by the Office of Technology Assessment and the National Institute of Mental Health brought together geneticists, psychiatrists, counselors, consumers, and patient advocates to explore the current state of research into the genetic aspects of mental disorders, in particular, the implications of genetic research for future management of psychiatric patients and the ethical and social issues surrounding this field.[13] The deliberations resulted in a landmark publication, *Mental Disorders and Genetics: Bridging the Gap Between Research and Society*.

Among the issues discussed was the demand of the general public for more detailed, precise information about the likelihood of developing mental disorders, as well as their potential impact on people's lives and available preventive opportunities. There was a general feeling that mental health professionals fail not only to adequately inform the public but also to educate themselves. Progress in genetic research of mental disorders is impressive, due mainly to rapid technological advances. However, immediate clinical applications are still limited, since specific genes in most mental disorders are yet to be identified and genetic tests and genetic therapy (i.e., genetic engineering) are still unavailable. Existing data point to the heterogeneous causation of mental disorders, involving both genetic and environmental factors; yet, simplistic, "nature v. nurture" sloganeering too frequently holds sway in media presentations.

Several ethical issues are involved in genetic counseling: possible social stigmatization; employment discrimination; inability to obtain or maintain medical insurance; and government social control of reproductive behavior of individuals with a known mental disorder or even of those who are merely carriers. On the personal level, we need to ask if a reliable blood test for depressive illness would lead affected people to decide not to have children. Given the delicacy of the situation and the fact that the problem of genetic transmission of depressive illness is very complex and not yet fully understood, genetic counseling should be done with the help of mental health professionals who are knowledgeable about the latest scientific advances.

On the basis of already available information, people of marriageable age should be informed about the phenomenon of "assortative mating," that is, the tendency of people to choose mates like themselves, so that those with affective disorder somehow find spouses with the same disorder. The children of such marriages are likely to develop affective disorders.[7,14] The odds of both nature and nurture are stacked against them.

The genetic counselor's role is to frankly and openly present both the known facts and the uncertainties to patients and their families, to inform them of the known risks, and to recognize that decisions in the presence of any particular set of odds are personal rather than medical. Such decisions should also be informed by the fast pace of psychobiological and drug research, already resulting in substantial amelioration in most cases of affective disorders, and by recognition that a cure at some future time is a distinct possibility.

None of the measures proposed in this chapter is new or revolutionary. What is needed now is a new resolve and willingness to commit our resources to massive intervention, as the only way to stem the tide of human misery. Can any public health measure make everyone happy and free of life's disappointments, losses, and disasters? Of course not. However, we can enable children to be more resilient and better prepared for whatever comes their way.

Our translation of biological principles into psychological preventive measures is less farfetched than it may at first appear. There is a growing consensus that any major progress in the prevention of depressive illness will evolve only from continued research and studies based on the intersection of neurochemistry, behavior, and genetics.

Cutting Edge

Major advances have been made in our understanding and treatment of childhood depression in the past decade. As we look to the future, we anticipate rapid strides, particularly in genetic research. In this chapter we review some of the major developments on the cutting edge of research into the causes and course of affective disorders.

Continuity or Discontinuity?

In earlier chapters we looked at the question of continuity and discontinuity in affective illness; that is, are these disorders seen and diagnosed in childhood identical to the disorders seen in adults? Although our sample of infants with bipolar parents was small, definite trends were evident. At the age of twelve months some infants of manic-depressive parents already showed disturbances in attachment behavior and dysregulation of affect. These became more pronounced with advancing age and appeared similar to the central characteristics of adults with affective illness. These characteristics include disturbed interpersonal relations marked by conflict, instability, and dissatisfaction. In addition, difficulties in handling emotions, particularly sadness and anger, and in maintaining emotional equilibrium were apparent.[1] The above characteristics found in such infants, toddlers, and adults may be related to the quintessential clinical features of depressive disorders: anhedonia and dysphoria.

By the age of five to six years, we can begin to make diagnoses of mood disorders using modified adult assessment instruments and unmodified adult diagnostic criteria. In addition to the clinical similarity, there are certain biological features that occur in varying degrees in both child and adult mood disorders, as previously mentioned. These include hypersecretion of cortisol in about 10 percent of children with major depressive disorder, diminished growth hormone response to an insulin tolerance test,[2] and diminished 24-hour MHPG excretion in the urine.[3]

It has been shown that many biological markers approximate adult values with advancing age, which suggests their developmental continuity.[4-6] We speculate that different subtypes of depressive illness are associated with biological markers that mature at different ages. Consequently, developmental studies of biological processes in children and adolescents may prove helpful in further illuminating the pathophysiology of affective disorders.[7]

Children with bipolar disorders respond to the same medication as do adults, while the response of unipolar children is still controversial and definitive studies are yet to be completed. There is a recent hopeful development, however; in July 1995, *Clinical Psychiatry News* reported on a well designed, double-blind study which clearly demonstrated the superiority of fluoxetine (Prozac) over placebo in children and adolescents with major depression. The results of the study, done by Dr. Graham Emslie of the University of Texas, Dallas, were similar to comparable reports in adults with major depression. If replicated, this study may represent a breakthrough in this contested field.[8] While bipolar (manic-depressive) disorder is relatively rare in childhood, there is well-documented evidence of good clinical response to lithium in children with this disorder.[9]

Compared to the rich if sometimes conflicting material available on the epidemiology of affective illness in adults, similar information on children is relatively scarce, particularly since children and adolescents have been excluded from the large epidemiological studies sponsored by the National Institutes of Health. However, a study of children in New Zealand, in which the authors collaborated, demonstrated the occurrence of depressive disorder in young children,[10] and many more recent studies indicate that the prevalence of mood disorders increases with age and approaches adult numbers in late adolescence.[11] Several follow-up studies indicate that (1) prepubertal mood disorders often continue into adolescence and adulthood,[12,13] (2) many children who develop depressive disorders in prepuberty will have at least one relapse before the age of fifteen,[14,15] and finally, (3) dysthymic disorder, the most common form of mood disorder in prepubertal children, frequently converts to major depressive disorder in adolescence, and usually has a protracted chronic course.[12] In fact, it has been suggested that early onset of a depressive disorder may foretell a more severe course of the illness, akin to that found in juvenile forms of rheumatoid arthritis and diabetes.[16,17]

The concept of discontinuity—that is, that affective disorders as seen in infancy and childhood are clinically similar to but fundamentally independent from those disorders in adulthood—finds limited support in the scientific literature. During infancy, depressive illness as we know it in older children and adults does not occur. However, when overwhelmed by life stresses of long duration, the infant may develop a primitive depressive state, characterized by a sad face, withdrawal, failure to interact, and even refusal of food.

Spitz described such extreme response to separation from mother in the second half of the first year as "anaclitic depression."[18] George Engel, in his famous study of Monica, named her affective withdrawal to threatening situations "conservation-withdrawal," which he conceptualized as a biological response akin to hibernation.[19] Finally Bowlby[20] in analyzing the behavior of children ages six months to three years who were separated from their mothers, noticed that, following a period of vigorous protest, there ensued a period he termed "despair," associated with social withdrawal, sad facial expression, whimpering, and refusal to eat. All the aforementioned disorders followed massive trauma.

In toddlers we still fail to see depressive illness diagnosable by standard operational criteria, although the possible precursors—difficulty with attachment behavior and affect dysregulation—do occur. We have found no studies, however, demonstrating a true and consistent link between such precursors and later adult affective illness.

Despite the fact that affective disorders can be properly diagnosed after the age of five, psychotic and manic states prior to adolescence are rarely seen. In contrast to the generally accepted higher prevalence of depression in females over males in adults (except in bipolar disorders), no such sex disparity has yet emerged from either epidemiological or offspring studies in children. Although suicidal ideation is frequently present in depressed children, suicidal attempts occur only rarely prior to adolescence.

Most of the issues reviewed concerning continuity and discontinuity probably can be explained from a developmental perspective. The absence of a true affective illness in infants and toddlers is probably due to cognitive and emotional immaturity. The lack of a sex disparity of affective illness prior to adolescence may be due to the fact that sex hormones, which exert a major influence on behavior at a later age, play a relatively minor role prior to adolescence. Alternatively, it may reflect the emergence, during adolescence, of strong differential socialization pressures for boys and girls.

In conclusion, the preponderance of evidence favors the concept of continuity of affective disorders in children, adolescence, and adults. This conclusion, coupled with the concept of kindling, discussed below, makes it imperative that we take childhood depression seriously and pursue more effective methods of prevention and treatment of this disorder.

The Kindling Phenomenon

According to Robert Post,[21] Emil Kraepelin realized already in the beginning of this century that in many patients with either unipolar and bipolar disorder the periods of well-being between successive episodes of affective illness became successively shorter. Kraepelin also noted that the initial episode of affective disorder was usually associated with or precipitated by a psychosocial stressor, while the subsequent episodes were less dependent on such triggering mechanism.[22] Many investigators have since confirmed these keen clinical observations for most bipolar and many unipolar patients. This was true before pharmacological treatment of these disorders was available—prior to the advent of antidepressant drugs—and is true even today. When patients are inadequately treated or are unresponsive to available medications, they continue to demonstrate the pattern of clinical deterioration, as the intervals between successive episodes of affective illness become progressively shorter.[23,24]

Kraepelin's other crucial observation, concerning the role of psychosocial stressors in the precipitation of affective illness, has been confirmed by a host of subsequent studies. The first episode of depression in a patient is usually associated with a severe psychosocial stressor, while only about one-third of patients experience such stressors in subsequent episodes. The severity of such psychosocial stressors progressively lessens as well, with each successive episode.[25,26] Such findings indicate that, while psychosocial factors play a crucial role in the onset of affective illness, their role in subsequent episodes becomes progressively less important, as the illness seems to become more autonomous and less dependent on external stressors.

Robert Post and his associates at the National Institute of Mental Health have proposed the "kindling phenomenon" as a theoretical model of the neurobiological events involved in recurrent affective disorders. "Kindling" is the progressively increasing responsivity of the brain to repeated electrical stimulation.[23,24]

In animal experiments, regularly repeated electrical stimulations of the brain lead to increasingly severe major motor seizures, evoked "by previously subthreshold stimulation. . . . [T]hese changes in the excitability of the brain tissue seem to be permanent and in time, with sufficient number of . . . kindled seizures, the animals develop spontaneous epilepsy, i.e., autonomous seizures in the absence of exogenous electrophysiological stimulation."[27] Post and his group believe that the phenomenon of electrical kindling may be pertinent to parallel processes "involved in the increasing vulnerability to relapse, demonstrated in some patients with recurrent affective illness."[21]

Kindling is characterized by permanent changes in brain function and structure. How can this happen? This is what we know so far: Kindling, like long-term memory, depends on protein synthesis. These proteins may involve cellular structures, such as enzymes, receptors, or structural proteins. Although proteins are constantly being turned over in the body, the changes brought on by kindling are permanent. How does the "kindling engram" remain immune to molecular turnover in the absence of additional, reminder seizures? Presumably some seizure-induced genetic mutation is required to maintain the long-term alteration thought to underlie the kindling process.[21]

In the past decade, scientists have begun to unravel the complex mechanisms by which extracellular signals may influence the genome. Much interest has been focused on a class of genes called "immediate-early genes" (IEGs). Their activation, in response to an appropriate stimulus, is rapid and transient. Their protein products bind to DNA and directly activate the expression of more durable genes, which are called "late effector genes" (LEGs). It is thought that these LEGs produce various proteins in the neuronal cell, such as receptors, enzymes, ion channels, peptides, and structural proteins.[28]

Because IEGs proteins are thought to turn on a developmental program by their activation of LEGs, IEGs are referred to as "master genes," whose job is to switch a cell from one genetic program to another. Recent studies have shown that in rats seizures involved in kindling are associated with changes in neuronal cell morphology, such as sprouting of mossy axons and dendrites, possibly forming new synaptic contacts (both axons and dendrites serve as the connections between neurons). These changes in cell morphology following kindling appear permanent and may lead to a kindled state, representing a durable memory trace.

The biochemical and morphological changes are referred to by Post and his colleagues[27,29] as "sculpting the central nervous system," akin to "formation of the basic wiring of the brain during development." They postulate that "related phases of neuroplasticity, synaptic reorganization, and neuronal tract sculpting could be occurring throughout adult life in relationship to processes of adaptation in response to an environmental impact."

Post deserves the credit for making the intellectual leap from the process of electrical kindling to a better understanding of processes involved in recurrent affective disorders. At first glance the two phenomena are quite different, since the process of electrical "kindling" and its behavioral correlates of seizure disorder seem to bear no resemblance to the symptoms of patients with affective disorders. Yet, Post and his group consider kindling "as a non-homologous model for the affective disorders and . . . a conceptual bridge, that might help describe the kind of neurobiological processes in the brain, that could be associated with the progression of a disorder."

This theoretical bridge, which links these two disparate phenomena, rests on two pillars that they share: (1) "increased behavioral responsivity to the same stimulation over time," and (2) "progression to spontaneity" following a sufficient number of repeated external stimulations.[30] In affective illness, psychosocial stress, particularly that related to separation, loss, and lowering of self-esteem, represents the requisite stimulus that triggers the recurrent episodes. According to Post, there are two related but separate operating mechanisms involved in this process. An affective episode may be triggered by a psychosocial stressor; moreover, the trigger may be provided by a previous affective episode. To carry the theoretical parallel further, an affective episode may be accompanied by intraneuronal functional and structural changes and may leave a permanent memory trace, which predisposes to further episodes; that is, "it is possible that episodes beget episodes."[21]

Of course, the validity of this theoretical formulation can be only established by demonstrating the activation of IEGs and LEGs and attendant neurobiological changes in response to a psychosocial stressor in brains of appropriate animal models or even in human beings. Amazing progress in the development of radiographic techniques makes this prospect realistic in the not too distant future.

Many Vietnam veterans suffer from post-traumatic stress disorder (PTSD). This may serve as a clinical example of the effect of severe emotional stress on function (and possibly structure) of part of the brain called amygdala. Dr. Dennis Charney, head of psychiatry at the Veterans Administration hospital in West Haven, Connecticut, has treated many Vietnam veterans with PTSD who suffered terrifying flashbacks. He comments, "It's been an eye-opener to me that individuals who were traumatized twenty-five years ago still show abnormal brain function. . . . [S]evere stress can change the way your brain functions biologically."[31] Interestingly, the amygdala was also used in the animal electrical kindling experiments that provided a model for Post's kindling theory.

According to neuroscientist Bruce McEwen of Rockefeller University, animal studies suggest that stress can switch genes on and off at the wrong times, forcing them to build abnormal networks of brain cell connections.[32] Several other studies have demonstrated that depressive illness and other types of chronic stress may cause permanent damage to the hippocampus, a crescent-shaped collection of neurons deep in the core of the brain involved in storing and retrieving memories.[33,34]

In addition to enhancing understanding of the nature of affective disorders, the kindling model has practical implications for the treatment and prevention of affective disorders. To begin with, it emphasizes the importance of preventing further episodes, since each one may increase the patient's vulnerability to future recurrences. Such reasoning strengthens the emerging consensus among clinicians that long-term and possibly lifelong drug therapy of both unipolar and bipolar disorders, beyond the duration of the acute episode, is the best protection against relapses.[21,35] The elucidation of the role of psychosocial stressors as possible triggers of the first episode of affective illness, which may set in motion a lifelong disorder, points to the importance of alleviating such stressors by early and vigorous psychosocial and maybe even pharmacological intervention. Finally, the clarification of the role of changes in genetic expression in affective illness may contribute to a better understanding of genetic factors in these disorders. Of course, at the end of the rainbow is the promise (mirage?) of therapeutic manipulation of the genetic expression, by inhibiting the relentless progression of the neurobiological changes underlying recurrent affective illness.

To date, Post's most important clinical contribution, based on the theoretical considerations of the kindling process, is his introduction of anticonvulsant medication as an effective alternative to lithium in bipolar disorders and a useful adjunct in many cases of unipolar disorder as well.[36]

Peter Levinson and his associates at the Oregon Research Institute have proposed an interesting psychosocial counterpoint to the kindling hypothesis. This involves psychological "scars" left after a first episode of depression in children and adolescents.[16,37,38] These aftereffects include internalizing behavior problems, excessive emotional reliance on others, more physical health problems, and subsyndromal depression symptoms. These investigators postulate that these psychological scars make adolescents more vulnerable "and are responsible for the high relapse rate of formerly depressed adolescents."

Gene Hunters

"The most important cartographers in the world these days don't work at Rand McNally or the CIA," writes Michael Schrage in *The Washington Post*.[39] He continues:

> They're not much interested in mountains and rivers and shifting national boundaries. In fact, they don't know much about traditional geography at all. . . . No, the influential map

makers of the 1990's ply their trade in molecular biology labs, charting the geography of genes. They're rapidly creating a veritable atlas of human, plant and animal genes, figuring out where individual genes are located and what they do.

This is proving to be one of the most productive ventures in the history of cartography: gene mapping is transforming biology, agriculture and medicine as surely as mapping the new world transformed Europe. This year alone [1994], researchers have located more that 45 new disease-producing genes in humans. This week, scientists announced the discovery of the gene that is believed to cause half of all inherited cases of breast cancer. This translates into a better than A-Gene-A-Week pace.

This pace is unlike anything medicine has witnessed before, as researchers fish genes out of cells at a dizzying rate. In 1993 we witnessed the discovery of more that a dozen genetic mutations responsible for diseases ranging from Alzheimer's to hyperactivity to colon cancer.

The advances leading to today's improved understanding of genetic factors started over forty years ago, when researchers found that the variability in the desoxyribonucleic acid (DNA), the essence of our genetic code, is deceptively simple and can be accounted for by the way four organic bases—adenine, guanine, thymine, and cytosine—are arrayed.[40] This discovery suddenly added sophistication to our rather primitive understanding of hereditary transmission, as imparted to us in the early 1860s by Gregory Mendel.

The eminent biogeneticist Samuel Barondes, from the University of California in San Francisco, estimates that the human genome—the sum total of all our genes—is composed of about three billion pairs of these organic bases. There are approximately 100,000 genes, which contain all the information needed to make each of us a distinctive individual. It is a truly herculean task to fully identify how each of the three billion of these organic base pairs translates the information contained in a genotype (the genetic endowment of a person, consisting of all genes received from each parent at a time of conception) into a phenotype (the outward, observable, and measurable expression of a person's genetic endowment). Fortunately, the enormous importance of this gigantic effort has been appropriately recognized and given special support in the so-called genome project started in the late 1980s by the National Institutes of Health. It is expected that even with all this effort it may be several decades before the entire human genome is mapped, each gene in its proper place or locus on the appropriate one of the forty-six chromosomes.

It is fascinating that even at these rather early stages there are impressive new genetic discoveries. An analogy here with the explorations of Vasco de Gama, Magellan, Champlain, and others would be quite fitting. They did not wait for perfect, detailed maps; in fact, they often made them up as they went along. The same happens with these bold, genetic explorers, who are eager to make their mark and earn their place in the annals of science.

Restriction Enzymes

What helped these investigators and gave them the necessary tools for exploration are the impressive advances in molecular genetics developed in the last two decades. Among the methodological advances that led to improved understanding of genetic diseases is the discovery of "restriction enzymes" by the Nobel prize winners Daniel Nathans and Hamilton O. Smith of Johns Hopkins University. These enzymes, first identified in bacteria, can excise fragments of DNA of varying length. Each enzyme predictably removes specific pieces, which allows the scientist to identify, isolate, and detach any desired fragment of the DNA. It is possible to correlate deviations from the expected DNA code sequence in a DNA segment with an anatomic or biochemical developmental defect. Such mutations become the genetic markers linked to specific disorders.

Polymerase Chain Reaction

Another important technological breakthrough in molecular genetics is the polymerase chain reaction, a method which allows scientists to study genetic mutations by making many exact copies of the mutation to provide investigators ample material with which to work. The techniques described above permit recognition of biochemical genetic diseases by examining the DNA from a single blood cell.

Gene Sequencing

Only three percent of the DNA contained in each human cell make up the actual 80,000–100,000 genes. The rest is called "junk" DNA. This makes the process of deciphering the genetic code of each DNA segment very tedious and time-consuming. It was the biochemist J. Craig Venter, formerly at the National Institutes of Health, who in 1990 came up with an ingenious idea that has revolutionized the field of gene mapping. DNA acts as the template for the formation of a corresponding ribonucleic acid (RNA) molecule, the so-called messenger RNA (MRNA).

Venter realized that he can use the relatively easy to isolate MRNA to make corresponding DNA copies. This saved the time-consuming intermediate step of separating the genes from the "junk" DNA. Next, he fed the DNA copies into a machine that uses robots for DNA sequencing—a process hitherto done manually. Such method was suggested in 1986 by a geneticist Leroy E. Hood. These sequencing machines, coupled with advanced supercomputers, dramatically cut the time of sequencing a code of an unknown gene and lowered the cost—from *50,000 dollars* (using old methods) to *20* dollars.[41]

Twin, family, and adoption studies strongly suggest that affective disorders may have a genetic component (see Chapter Five).[22] This gave impetus during the 1980s to efforts of several psychogenetic investigators to search for a gene causing manic-depressive (bipolar) disorder. Bipolar illness was chosen because of (1) the clear-cut nature of its symptoms, which makes it easier to distinguish patients with this disorder, and (2) the relative high concordance of monozygotic twins with bipolar illness (up to 75 percent in some studies), which suggested a strong genetic contribution.[42] Encouraged by spectacular successes in identifying many genetic disorders in internal medicine, neurological disorders and oncology, psychiatric researchers hoped to find a gene for bipolar disorder in patients from families with a high incidence of this illness. They used linkage analysis studies—that is, the search for genetic markers—which may disclose the location of a gene on a particular chromosome. In the 1980s, before the spectacular advances in molecular genetics, these linkage studies used physical characteristics or biological factors as genetic markers if they were inherited by patients with bipolar disorder. If a bipolar disorder and such a genetic marker occurred consistently in the same individual, one could assume that these conditions were linked and occupied neighboring genetic loci, and once such locus was known, the gene for bipolar disorder should be located nearby. Such a genetic marker, applied to each individual in a pedigree (family ancestry), would successfully predict who was at risk and who was not.

Using this methodology, Rieder and Gershon[43] proposed certain criteria for a genetic marker of vulnerability to an illness:

1. The characteristic must be associated with an increased likelihood of the psychiatric illness.
2. It must be heritable and not be a secondary effect of the illness. Phenomena that are demonstrable only in the presence of active illness are of limited usefulness in genetic investigation of an illness with incomplete penetrance. For example, if a urinary metabolite is decreased only during episodes of illness, it would be impossible to determine whether well relatives or controls would have the same findings.
3. It must be observable (or evocable) in the well state, so that it is possible to determine its presence independently of the illness and to evaluate well relatives.

This approach proved rather futile for manic-depressive disorder, with many dramatic, highly publicized findings that could not be replicated. Among the early, unsuccessful "candidates" for a genetic marker in bipolar disorder were: color blindness, XG blood group, glucose-6-phosphate dehydrogenase (G6PD) deficiency, human leukocyte antigen (HLA), monoamine metabolism (enzymes and metabolite), cholinergic pharmacological response and receptor density, plasma GABA, and (3H) imipramine binding related to serotonin transport. All of these linkage studies have had controversial results. Either the data have not proven to be replicable or they have lacked statistical significance.[44]

When the modern techniques made it possible to examine specific DNA fragments, scientists realized that such fragments could be used as markers in linkage analysis if they showed deviations from the normal nucleotide (DNA) sequence. Normally, there are slight variations (polymorphisms) in these nucleotide sequences, the vast majority of which do not cause any functional abnormalities. In the last ten years, many such polymorphic DNA fragments have been isolated and identified in specific locations on the human genome.

One of the most famous studies using such modern techniques of genetic linkage was reported by Janice Egeland and her group at Miami University.[45] This report linked a large mutated DNA fragment on chromosome 11 with manic-depressive illness in a large Amish family in Pennsylvania. The researchers claimed that this pattern of genetic transmission conformed to simple Mendelian patterns and involved a single dominant gene. This discovery was hailed as a breakthrough in behavioral research, promising to serve as an example and catalyst for other studies of psychiatric disorders.

Egeland's results, based on identification of inherited bipolar disease in thirty-two families, were bolstered by the statistical analysis of the data, which indicated that the odds that the linkage between this DNA marker and bipolar disorder was accidental were very slight (between 1 in 10,000 and 1 in 100,000). However, within a very short time after this publication, the enthusiasm over this landmark study gave way to bitter disappointment. The reason for such an unfortunate turn of events indicates the pitfalls of statistical analysis in genetic research. What demolished the seemingly rock solid data was the fact that *only two individuals,* neither of whom possessed the genetic marker and both of whom were healthy at the time of the study, developed full-blown symptoms of manic-depressive illness. These occurrences suddenly lowered the odds of the original findings being accidental to less than 1 in 10.[41]

Another study, by Miron Baron from Columbia University and his associates in Israel, linked bipolar disorder with a region on the X chromosome. It suffered a similarly quick demise when the findings could not be replicated.[41]

These highly publicized failures had the effect of discouraging "triumphal" announcements of preliminary findings, akin to "jumping the gun" in a race, and encouraging a more cautious approach to the study of genetic linkage in bipolar illness. Many researchers concluded that, rather than try to gamble on the possibility of quick victory by focusing on a single "interesting" segment of DNA, they would undertake the very difficult but more promising approach of scanning the entire genome first, looking for promising DNA markers. The advocates of such an elaborate, labor intensive effort argue that such a complex behavioral disturbance as manic-depressive illness is unlikely to be linked to only one gene; rather, it may be multifactorial (the result of an interaction of several genes). David Cox of Stanford University says "that focusing on individual genetic loci that give an appearance of linkage to manic-depressive illness may be likened to the use of a small net to snag a fish out of a pool, when it would be better to drain the pool and collect all the fish from the bottom. Doing whole genome scan—though more time-consuming—is like draining the pool."[41]

At present, most genetic researchers combine the techniques of scanning the entire genome with targeting and investigating individual promising "candidates" for single genes.

While this fascinating search continues, and still has elements of a race involving research teams in the USA, Canada and Europe, investigators today are more "gun-shy" and extremely cautious about publishing their findings. When they do publish, they prudently include many potentially face-saving caveats. In a 1994 publication of interesting findings involving linkage of bipolar disorder with a DNA marker on chromosome 18, Elliot Gershon from National Institute of Mental Health and Wade Berrettini from Jefferson University reported that bipolar illness may have a very complex mode of inheritance, being dominant in some families and recessive in others.[46] Gershon believes that different mutations of one gene or environmental effects on disease expression are possible explanations for these differences in the mode of inheritance.

And so the quest continues—for the cause and eventually the cure of one of mankind's major mental afflictions.

From Tabula Rasa to Behavioral Determinism— The Perennial Nature-Nurture Controversy

The controversy about the role of inborn biological factors versus the environmental influences on human normal and abnormal behavior has often pitted extremists on both sides of the argument against each other. The proponents of the primacy of environment predominated in American psychiatry and psychology until well into the middle of the twentieth century.

The behaviorists of that time, as epitomized by the extreme views of J.B. Watson, the "Father" of behaviorism, believed that the destiny of a child, whether he grows up a creative genius or a criminal, depends completely on his or her upbringing and conditioning in childhood. In other words, the people in the child's environment, be they parents or teachers, can mold the child's personality into any desired pattern.

These extreme beliefs, derived from the studies of conditioned reflexes in Pavlov's and Skinner's animal experiments, found ready acceptance by the American public, dedicated as it is to the idea that "All men are created equal," and if given a "chance," that is, the optimal environmental input, their possibilities for a successful life and career are virtually limitless, regardless of their natural endowment. This, of course, contrasted sharply with the old world view, that each man "was born to his station." As Bruno Bettelheim wrote:

The Freudian views on human development seriously competed with behaviorism for public acceptance. The psychoanalytic school gave due recognition to the permanence of much of our evolutionary inheritance, while at the same time stressing the importance of early experiences that can modify the way our inherited characteristics will be shaped and expressed in our personality.[47]

The balance of forces shifted dramatically during the last few decades, as the importance of biological and, in particular, genetic influences became increasingly accepted. The psychiatric community was at first rather late in recognizing these influences. It is difficult to believe today that as late as 1976 autism was attributed to the malignant influence of "refrigerator" mothers and considered unlikely to be genetic in nature.[48] Schizophrenia was believed to be caused by abnormal parenting even in the 1960s, when the concept of a "schizophrenogenic" mother was in vogue.

The acceptance of the crucial role of genetic factors in human behavior accelerated dramatically in the 1970s and 1980s, spurred by adoption and twin studies and the spectacular advances in molecular genetics. In many instances, the pendulum swung too much in this direction, leading many behavioral scientists to confine the environmental influences on behavior to the scrap heap of "has-been" theories. As an example, Seligman, the same scientist who conceived of the concept of learned helplessness—an environmentally caused condition par excellence—denies, in his most recent writings,[49] that human beings are scarcely creatures of our upbringing and culture at all. He further concludes that any childhood trauma is barely detectable in adulthood. "If you want to blame your parents for your own adult problems," says Seligman, "you are entitled to blame the genes they gave you, but you are not entitled—by any facts I know—to blame the way they treated you. . . . childhood contrary to popular belief does not seem, empirically, to be particularly formative." And later, "In no way are childrearing practices likely to even enhance a genetic predisposition." These extreme views are buttressed not by the author's painstaking research, which he did so admirably in his work on "learned helplessness," but, rather, by referencing supportive studies without much detail.[50]

Since the genetic theories of behavior are now "flying high," there is no need for us to marshall forces in their defense, especially since we have covered the topic extensively elsewhere in the book. There is, however, a need to come to the aid of the presently embattled, besieged role of environmental influences on human behavior.

To the objective mind, it is obvious that changes in environmental conditions may alter the expression of a genetic predisposition: children, heterozygous for sickle cell anemia, are usually free of symptoms at sea level, but may develop sickling at higher altitudes. Likewise, phenylketonuria leads to severe mental retardation if the afflicted children eat a normal diet; however, mental retardation can be prevented or minimized by environmental manipulation, that is, restriction of dietary phenylalanine. Type I (what used to be called juvenile) diabetes may serve as another example. There is plenty of evidence that people who develop this form of diabetes harbor a genetic predisposition for the disease. Recently, Massimo Trucco and his associates at Children's Hospital in Pittsburgh discovered compelling evidence that a viral infection triggers this severe illness by causing the immune system to overreact and destroy vital insulin-producing cells in the pancreas.[51] Scientists even speculate that this discovery, if confirmed, may eventually lead to the development of a vaccine for people with a family history of diabetes.

The aforementioned conditions are relatively simple in comparison to the complex polygenic factors that interact with environmental influences to determine personality characteristics or psychiatric illness. However, the logic remains the same.

Robert Plomin, one of our foremost behavioral geneticists, states it succinctly:[52]

> Genetics research provides the best evidence for the importance of nonheritable factors. As convincing as twin and adoption studies are, the genetic factors do not account for

more than about half of the variance for behavioral disorders and dimensions, and most of the disorders . . . show as much nonheritable as heritable influences. . . . The current enthusiasm for genetics should not obscure the important contribution of nonheritable factors, even though they are much more difficult to investigate.

Plomin and his group have contributed one of the most important concepts for the understanding of environmental influences—the idea of "nonshared environment." "The fact that psychopathology often runs in families has reasonably but wrongly been interpreted to indicate that psychopathology is not under environmental control. We know now that each member of a family is exposed to a different set of influences, attitudes and circumstances."[52] Such disparate environmental experiences may explain the curious phenomenon that identical twins, growing up in the same family, may be discordant for major mental illness, such as depression or schizophrenia.[53,54]

Although adoption studies generally lend support to the role of genetic factors in depressive disorders, a study by Knorring, Cloninger and associates[55] reported that over 90 percent of depressed adoptees in their sample, most of whom were diagnosed as having nonpsychotic major depression, had no biological parent known to have a depressive disorder. A study of the so-called "cohort effect" in relatives from the NIMH psychobiology of depression collaborative program provides more evidence for the importance of environmental factors in affective disorders; Gerald Klerman and his associates found a striking increase of major depression in each of the succeeding younger birth cohorts born since World War II.[56] These findings parallel those found on alcoholism, suicide, and bipolar disorder and cannot be thought as merely the result of changes in genetic susceptibility factors.

Dinwiddie[57] has suggested that "by controlling for genetic factors (e.g., in twin study designs), the use of behavioral genetic techniques should allow researchers to identify environmental risk factors and characterize their influences on different genotypes with a high degree of precision." In a recent, elegant, pioneering study of 680 female homozygous and heterozygous twins, Kendler and his associates[58] attempted to investigate the interconnection of nine possible predictive variables of major depression: genetic factors, parental warmth, childhood parental loss, lifetime traumas, neuroticism, social support, past depressive episodes, recent difficulties, and recent traumatic life events. The strongest predictors of liability to major depression were, in descending order: (1) stressful life events, (2) genetic factors, (3) previous history of major depression, and (4) neuroticism. The authors conclude that major depression is a multifactorial disorder, and understanding its etiology will require the rigorous integration of genetic, temperamental, and environmental risk factors.

As our brief review of behavioral genetics indicates, there are many unresolved issues on both sides of the argument, mainly because the research methodology has lagged behind boldly expressed hypotheses. As sensible people in both the environmental and genetic camps valiantly struggle to improve their methods, using integrated, multifactorial, etiological research designs, we will get closer to unraveling the many causal pathways to major depression. In the meantime, it might be wise to scale down the rhetoric pending further developments in the burgeoning field of behavioral genetics.

Neuroimaging: A Window on the Human Brain

The centrality of the brain in human emotion was not recognized until the latter part of the nineteenth century. Aristotle, whom many regard as the father of biology in the Western tradition, correctly described the location and consistency of the brain, but believed that its only function was to cool and moderate the heart, the latter being the central organ of sense and feeling: "The motions of pain and pleasure, and generally of all sensation plainly start from the heart and find in it their ultimate termination. . . . the brain then tempers the heat and seething of the heart."[59] The idea of the heart being the seat of emotions persisted through the ages, only occasionally competing with the liver and the spleen. This may explain the expressions "heart-broken," "lily-livered," and "venting one's spleen."[60]

Paul Broca,[61] the French pathologist, anthropologist, and pioneer in neurosurgery, was first to describe an area of the brain below the cerebral cortex, which included the cingulate, hippocampus, and paraolfactory areas. Broca named the area "the limbic lobe," since it *borders* the brainstem (*limbus* being the Latin term for border). Later, other structures were added, notably the amygdala, septum, thalamus, and hypothalamus.[62] It was not until the twentieth century that Papez[63] and MacLean[64] conceived the idea of the limbic loop (circle) and proposed it as the seat of human emotions. These ideas became generally accepted despite lacking direct, supportive evidence.

Recently, the emergence of the novel science of brain imaging has permitted a detailed visualization of brain structures and their function in the living brain (in vivo). This new field can be divided into three major areas: (1) the structural (anatomical), examination of the brain, (2) the functional evaluation of different brain areas, and (3) visualization of molecular brain structures, such as receptors and neurotransmitters.

Heralding this exciting era of discovery was the introduction in 1973 of computerized axial tomography (CT scan), conceived by Godfrey Hounsfield. This technique uses multiple exposures of standard x-rays, directed at many angles of the brain. The images, reconstructed by a computer, offer a higher resolution than conventional single x-ray film. CT scanning allows the visualization of virtually all parts of the body—their localization and structure but not their function. A powerful competitor to the CT scan appeared in the 1980s in the form of magnetic resonance imaging (MRI), which utilizes nuclear magnetic resonance (NMR) technology, independently discovered in 1946 by two physicists, Purcell and Bloch, who jointly won the Nobel Prize in 1952.[65] The main advantages of the MRI over CT include (1) no ionizing radiation and (2) better quality imaging without the use of contrast injections.[66]

Other functional neuroimaging techniques include positron emission tomography (PET) and single photon emission computerized tomography (SPECT), both of which measure cerebral blood flow as an index of brain activity. There is substantial evidence that a local elevation in human-brain blood oxygenation correlates with increased neuronal activity.[67,68]

A recent magnetic resonance imaging (MRI) technique takes advantage of the difference in magnetic properties of oxygenated versus deoxygenated blood. The oxyhemoglobin in oxygen-rich blood is attracted by a magnet, while deoxyhemoglobin in oxygen-poor blood is slightly repelled by a magnet. This phenomenon, termed BOLD for blood-oxygenation-level-dependent contrast, allows the measurement of oxygen utilization, which reflects the activity of the brain or other tissues.[69-71] It is comparable to the deoxyglucose PET scan, but has great advantages over the latter: (1) it is totally non-invasive, (2) it requires no radioactive contrast material, (3) there is no ionizing radiation, and (4) the duration of the procedure is ten to fifteen times shorter than the PET scan.[72] This new technique is particularly well suited for functional neuroimaging in children; along with MRI spectroscopy it offers exciting possibilities for this age group.[69]

The neuroreceptors can now be imaged in vivo in the human brain by using PET scanning. These images may provide valuable information about (1) the number and distribution of the receptors in the central nervous system (CNS), (2) the concentration of neurotransmitters at the synapse, and (3) the affinity of a receptor for a specific drug. These techniques open great opportunities to enhance our knowledge of brain neurochemistry in healthy and psychiatrically ill people. Moreover, they can help in monitoring drug action and effectiveness, as well as in the search for new pharmacological agents.[73]

Magnetic resonance spectroscopy (MRS) has been introduced to study important metabolites in living tissues, including the brain. It is related to MRI and also based on the discovery of nuclear magnetic resonance (NMR). This non-invasive method has already yielded information on brain metabolism and energy production, as well as protein and amino acid metabolism. It can also be used to study the action of psychopharmacological agents. Ongoing technological improvements will no doubt broaden the range of applications and make MRS a serious competitor to older methods, such as PET and SPECT, which are invasive and/or involve radiation exposure.[74] The development of these varied functional neuroimaging methods finally has helped to "breach the biological limitations imposed by the inaccessibility of the human brain."[75]

Several excellent reviews have summarized the recent status of neuroimaging in child psychiatry.[66,76,77] All decry the still limited use of neuroimaging techniques in this age group, especially that of functional neuroimaging. The main impediment to the use of the neuroimaging techniques in children lies in ethical concerns about the safety of these innovations, which involve ionizing radiation and injection of radioactive substances. CT scan, PET, and SPECT all share in these drawbacks. Although magnetic resonance (MR) techniques for structural and functional neuroimaging do not have ionizing radiation and do not use radioactive materials, there are still concerns about their safety in children. To begin with, sedation in children is usually required during such procedures, and some experts worry about the potential dangers of exposure to a high magnetic field. The amazingly rapid progress and constant improvements in magnetic resonance techniques offer the best hope for increased future safety, which would open the door for a wider use in youngsters, both in research and clinical practice.[78]

Mark George and his associates at the National Institute of Mental Health recently reported a landmark study of changes in regional cerebral blood flow associated with experimentally evoked transient sadness or happiness in healthy adult women. In addition to validating the involvement of the limbic system in human emotions, the study also demonstrated the involvement of other brain structures, including the brainstem, basal ganglia, and some regions of the cerebral cortex. The investigators have found that different emotions affect different parts of the brain. Sadness was generally associated with increased brain activity, while during transient happiness this activity decreased (See Figure).[79]

How the Brain Computes Tears and Laughter

The brain handles happiness and sadness in different areas, not in a single emotional center as was thought. New fast scanning methods show that happiness is marked by a decrease in activity in the cortex, in areas responsible for forethought and planning. Sadness is associated with enhanced activity in regions of the limbic system. PET scans below show changes in activity of subjects experiencing the two emotional states.

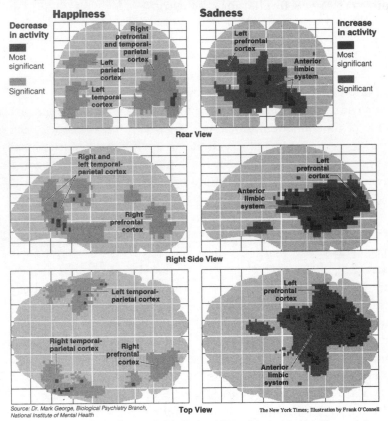

Source: Dr. Mark George, Biological Psychiatry Branch, National Institute of Mental Health

The New York Times; Illustration by Frank O'Connell

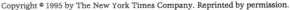

In commenting on the above study, George Robinson from the University of Iowa expressed the belief that direct identification of brain structures that mediate normal emotions may enable us to study these same structures in patients with various psychiatric disorders. "We could also examine whether either psychotherapeutic or pharmacological treatments could alter the anatomical or physiological processes involved in mediation of emotion. Perhaps the ultimate benefit . . . from this line of investigation, however, is the ability to develop targeted rational therapies. . . . this work represents a pathway to an exciting and provocative new frontier for psychiatry."[62]

Epilogue

Joy is an emotion by which the body's power of action is increased or assisted. Sorrow, on the other hand, is an emotion by which the body's power of action is lessened or restrained, and therefore joy is . . . good; sorrow on the other hand is . . . evil.

Baruch Spinoza (1632–1677)

At a 1993 meeting of the American Group Psychotherapy Association in San Diego, Joel Yager, professor of psychiatry at UCLA, predicted profound, fundamental changes in mental health clinical practice fifty years hence, in 2043.[1] These changes will be driven by: the ongoing rapid progress in neuroscience, developmental psychopathology, mental health outcome research, and health economics, which will force better accountability and more specific, reliable, targeted therapeutic interventions. These will replace the still prevalent multitude of treatment modalities—the choice of which largely depends on the popularity of a given "therapy du jour."

Yager singled out one recent scientific finding of Lewis Baxter: a decrease in originally elevated metabolic rates in the right caudate nucleus in successfully treated patients with obsessive compulsive disorder (OCD). The metabolic normalization, as seen in positron-emission tomography (PET) scans,[2] occurred whether the patients were successfully treated with behavior or drug therapy. According to Yager, such findings will convince even the bill-paying skeptics in managed care of the importance of psychosocial intervention, not as an amorphous, hard to measure therapeutic modality, but, rather, as one that produces a measurable change in brain functioning.

In the office of the future, the child with an affective disorder is likely to be referred to a radiologist to determine his or her structural and functional brain characteristics, including the localization of brain activity, the status of neuroreceptors, neuronal cell structures, and neurotransmitter distribution. Genetic testing of the patient and his close family members will follow. Such neurobiological analysis will help to pinpoint the exact nature of any given subtype of the presenting disorder and facilitate a targeted, precise choice of therapeutic intervention, be it pharmacological or psychotherapeutic.

Recent biological advances lead many to believe that the future of psychiatry depends solely on neuroscientific advances. Such views, in our opinion, are shortsighted and fail to encompass the complexity of human behavior. Rather, the mental health clinic of the future will also offer social skills training, crisis intervention, grief and divorce counseling, parent and teacher effectiveness training, and other modalities aimed at strengthening the emotional resilience of the child and his family. Such a comprehensive biopsychosocial approach will ensure the necessary *remedicalization* of psychiatry, while preventing its *dehumanization*.

Finally, we should like to repeat the closing remarks in our earlier book, *Why Isn't Johnny Crying?*, which are as timely now as they were in the early 1980s.

Early detection and treatment of depressed children, before the depression becomes a way of life, is essential.

Given timely and appropriate help, most depressed children can be helped to live a normal and productive life.

Endnotes

Chapter One

1. Cytryn, L., Cytryn, E., Rieger, R. Psychological implications of cryptorchism. In: Chess, S., Thomas, A., eds. *Annual Progress in Child Psychiatry and Child Development*. New York: Brunner/Mazel; 1968: 396–419.
2. Cytryn L. Factors in psychosocial adjustment of children with chronic illness and handicaps. *Clinical Proceedings*, Children's Hospital, Washington, DC. 1971;28:85–90.
3. Cytryn, L., Moore, P.V.P., Robinson, M.E. Psychological adjustment of children with cystic fibrosis. In: Anthony, E.J., Koupernick, L.C., eds. *The Child and His Family*. New York: Wiley; 1973.
4. Robins, L.N., Regier, D.A. *Psychiatric Disorders in America: The Epidemiological Catchment Area Study*. New York: Free Press; 1991.
5. McKnew, D.H., Cytryn, L., Efron, A.M., Gershon, E.S., Bunney, W.E. Offspring of manic-depressive patient. *British Journal of Psychiatry*. 1979; 134:148.
6. Fleming, J.E., Offord, D.R. Epidemiology of childhood depressive disorders: A critical review. *Journal of the American Academy of Child and Adolescent Psychiatry*. 1990;29:571–58.

Chapter Two

1. Kline, N.S. *From Sad to Glad*. New York: Ballantine; 1974.
2. Weinberg, W.A., Rutman, J., Sullivan, L., Penick, E.C., Dietz, S.G. Depression in children referred to an educational diagnostic center: Diagnosis and treatment. *Journal of Pediatrics*. 1973;83:1065.
3. Cytryn, L., McKnew, D.H., Jr. Proposed classification of childhood

depression. In: Chess, S., Thomas, A., eds. *Annual Progress in Child Psychiatry and Child Development.* New York: Brunner/Mazel; 1973: 419–432.

4. Cytryn, L., McKnew, D.H. Diagnosis of depression in children: A reassessment. In: Chess, S., Thomas, A. eds. *Annual Progress in Child Psychiatry and Child Development.* New York: Brunner/Mazel; 1981: 581–589.

5. Cytryn, L., McKnew, D.H. Factors influencing the changing clinical expression of the depressive process in children. In: Chess, S., Thomas, A. eds. *Annual Progress in Child Psychiatry and Child Development.* New York: Brunner/Mazel; 1975.

6. Freud, A. *The Ego and the Mechanisms of Defense.* New York: International Universities Press; 1946.

7. Kashani, J.H., Silva, P.A., Anderson, J.C., Clarkson, S.E., McGee, R.O., Walton, L.A., Williams, S.M., Robins, A.J., Cytryn, L., McKnew, D.H. The nature and prevalence of major and minor depression in a sample of nine-year-old children. *Archives of General Psychiatry.* 1983; 40:1217–1227.

8. Geller, B., Fox, L., Clark, B.A. Rate and predictors of prepubertal bipolarity during follow-up of six-to-twelve year old depressed children. *Journal of the American Academy of Child and Adolescent Psychiatry.* 1994;33:461–468.

9. Weinberg, W.A., Brumback, R.H. Mania in childhood. *Archives of American Journal of Diseases of Children.* 1976; 130:380.

10. Hodges, K., Kline, J., McKnew, D.H., Cytryn, L. The development of a child assessment interview for research and clinical use. *Journal of Abnormal Child Psychology.* 1992; 10:173–180.

11. Herjanic, B. Diagnostic interview for children and adolescents (DICA). Available from B. Herjanic, Washington University School of Medicine, St. Louis, MO, 1977.

12. Kovacs, M. Interview Schedule for Children (ISC) Form C. Unpublished manuscript. Available from M. Kovacs, Western Psychiatric Institute and Clinic, Pittsburgh, PA, 1983.

13. Chambers, W., Puig-Antich, J., Hisch, M. et al. The assessment of affective disorders in children and adolescents by semistructured interview. *Archives of General Psychiatry.* 1985;42:696–702.

Chapter Three

1. Weissman, M.M., Leckman, J.R., Merikangas, K.R., Jammon, G.D., Prusoff, B.A. Depression and anxiety disorder in parents and children: Results from the Yale Family Study. *Archives of General Psychiatry.* 1984;41:845–852.

2. Weissman, M.M., Leaf, P.J., Tischler. Affective disorders in five United States communities. *Psychological Medicine.* 1988;18:141–153.

3. Robins, L.N., Regier, D.A. *Psychiatric Disorders in America: The Epidemiological Catchment Area Study*. New York: Free Press; 1991.

4. Bridges, K.N.B. Emotional development in early infancy. *Child Development.* 1932;3:324–341.

5. Izard, C.E. On the development of emotions and emotion-cognition relationships in infancy. In: Lewis, M. Rosenbloom, L.A., eds. *The Development of Affect*. New York: Plenum Press, 1978;389–413.

6. Lazarus, R.S., Canner, A.D., Folkman, S. Emotions: A cognitive-phenomenological analysis. In: Plutchik, R., Kellerman, H., eds. *Theories of Emotion, Vol. I*. New York: Academic Press; 1980: 189–217.

7. Brazelton, T.B., Koslowski, B., Main, M. The origin of reciprocity; the early mother-infant interaction. In: Lewis, M. Rosenbloom, L.A., eds. *The Effect of the Infant on Its Caregiver*. New York: Wiley; 1974: 49–74.

8. Spitz, R.A. Autoerotism examined: The role of early sexual behavior patterns in personality formation. *Psychoanalytic Study of the Child.* 1962;17:283–315.

9. Mahler, M.S., Pine, F., Bergman, A., eds. *The Psychological Birth of the Human Infant*. New York: Basic Books; 1975.

10. Solnit, A.J. Developmental perspectives on self and object constancy. *Psychoanalytic Study of the Child.* 1982;32:201–217.

11. Mahler, M.S. Rapprochement subphase of the separation-individuation process. *Psychoanalytic Quarterly.* 1972;41:487–506.

12. Lewis, H.B. Shame in depression and hysteria. In: Izard, C., ed. *Emotions in Personality and Psychopathology*. New York: Plenum Press; 1979;369–396.

13. Spitz, R.A., Wolf, K.M. Anaclitic depression: An inquiry into the genesis of psychiatric condition on early childhood. *Psychoanalytic Study of the Child.* 1946;2:313–342.

14. Bowlby, J. *Attachment Vol. I*. New York: Basic Books; 1969.

15. Ainsworth, M., Blehar, M.C., Waters, E. *Patterns of Attachment: A Psychological Study of the Strange Situation*. Hillsdale, NJ: Erlbaum; 1978.

16. Schaeffer, H.R., Callender, W.M. Psychological effects of hospitalization in infancy. *Pediatrics.* 1959;24:528–539.

17. Thomas, A., Chess, S. *Temperament and Development*. New York: Brunner/Mazel; 1977.

18. Chess, S., Thomas, A. *Origins and Development of Behavioral Disorders*. New York: Brunner/Mazel; 1984.

19. Lerner, J.A. The import of temperament for psychosocial functioning: tests of goodness of fit model. *Merrill-Palmer Quarterly.* 1984;30: 177–188.

20. Kagan, J., Reznick, J.S., Clarke, C., Sidman, N., Garcia-Coll, C. Behavior inhibition to the unfamiliar. *Child Development.* 1984;55: 2212–2225.

21. Resnick, G.S., Kagan, J., Snidman, N., Gosten, M., Baak, K., Rosenberg, A. Inhibited and uninhibited children: A follow-up study. *Child Development.* 1986;57:660–680.

22. Kagan, J. *The Nature of the Child.* New York: Basic Books; 1984.

23. Rosenbaum, J.F., Biederman, J., Gerston, M., Hirshfeld, D.R., Meminger, S.R., Herman, J.B., Kagan, J., Reznick, J.S., Snidman, N. Behavioral inhibition in children of parents with panic disorder and agoraphobia. *Archives of General Psychiatry.* 1988;45:463–470.

24. Biederman, J., Rosenbaum, J.F., Hirshfeld, D.R., Faraone, S.V., Bolduc, E.A., Gerston, M., Meminger, S.R., Kayon, J., Snidman, N., Resnick, J.S. Psychiatric correlates of behavioral inhibitions in young children of parents with and without psychiatric disorders. *Archives of General Psychiatry.* 1990;47:21–26.

25. Cytryn, L., McKnew, D.H., Zahn-Waxler, C., Radke-Yarrow, M., Gaensbauer, T.J., Harmon, R.J., Lamour, M. Affective disturbances in the offspring of affectively ill patients–a developmental view. *American Journal of Psychiatry.* 1984;141:219–222.

26. Gaensbauer, T.J., Harmon, R.J. Clinical assessment in infancy utilizing structured playroom situations. *Journal of American Academy of Child Psychiatry.* 1981;20:264–280.

27. Harmon, R.J., Culp, A.M. The effect of premature birth on family functioning and infant development. In: Berlin, I. ed. *Children in Our Future.* Albuquerque: University of New Mexico Press; 1981.

28. Zahn-Waxler, C., McKnew, D.H., Cummings, E.M, Davenport, Y.B, Radke-Yarrow, M. Problem behaviors and peer interactions of young children with a manic-depressive parent. *American Journal of Psychiatry.* 1984;141:236–240.

29. Zahn-Waxler, C., Mayfield, A., Radke-Yarrow, M., McKnew, D.H., Cytryn, L., Davenport, Y.B. A follow-up investigation of offspring of parents with bipolar disorder. *American Journal of Psychiatry.* 1988; 145:506–509.

30. Spitzer, L., Endicott, J., Robins, E. Research diagnostic criteria. *Archives of General Psychiatry.* 1972;35:773–782.

31. Cytryn, L., McKnew, D.H., Sherman, T. Psychopathological syndromes in toddlers. Presented at the 140th Annual Meeting of the American Psychiatric Association. Chicago, 1987.

32. Radke-Yarrow, M., Nottleman, E., Martinez, P., Fox, M.B., Belman, B. Young children of affectively ill parents: longitudinal study of psychosocial development. *Journal of the American Academy of Child and Adolescent Psychiatry.* 1992;31:68–77.

33. Bakwin, H. Emotional deprivation in infants. *Journal of Pediatrics.* 1949;35:512–521.

34. Engel, G.L. Anxiety and depression withdrawal: The primary affects of unpleasure. *International Journal of Psychoanalysis.* 1962;43:89.

Chapter Four

1. National Center for Health Statistics Advance report of final mortality statistics, 1991. *Monthly Vital Statistics Report.* Hyattsville, MD: Public Health Service, 1992, 40(13).
2. *Wall Street Journal,* April 21, 1995.
3. Andrus, J.K., Fleming, D.N., Neumann, M.A., Wassell, J.T., Hopkins, D.D., Gordon, J. Surveillance of attempted suicide among adolescents in Oregon, 1991. *American Journal of Public Health.* 1991;81: 1067–1069.
4. Kline, N.S. *From Sad to Glad.* New York: Ballantine Books; 1974.
5. Pfeffer, C.R., Conte, H.R., Plutchik, R., Jerrett, I. Suicidal behavior in latency-age children: An empirical study. *Journal of the American Academy of Child Psychiatry.* 1979;18:679.
6. Pfeffer, C.R., Conte, H.R., Plutchik, R., Jerrett, I. Suicidal behavior in latency-age children: An outpatient population. *Journal of the American Academy of Child Psychiatry.* 1980;19:703.
7. Pfeffer, C.R., Klerman, G.L., Hurt, S.W., Kakuma, T., Peskin, J.R., Siefker, C.A. Suicidal children grow up: Rates and psychosocial risk factors for suicide attempts during follow-up. *Journal of the American Academy of Child and Adolescent Psychiatry.* 1993;30:106–113.
8. Kovacs, M., Goldston, D., Gatsonis, C. Suicidal behaviors and childhood-onset depressive disorders: A longitudinal investigation. *Journal of the American Academy of Child and Adolescent Psychiatry.* 1993;32:8–20.
9. Pfeffer, C.R. *The Suicidal Child.* New York: Guilford, 1986.
10. Cytryn, L., McKnew, D.H., Zahn-Waxler, C., Radke-Yarrow, M., Gaensbauer, T.J., Harmon, R.J. Affective disturbances in the offspring of affectively ill patients—a developmental view. *American Journal of Psychiatry.* 1984;141:219–222.
11. Shaffer, D., Fisher, P. The epidemiology of suicide in children and young adolescents. *Journal of the American Academy of Child Psychiatry.* 1981;21:545.
12. Puig-Antich, J., Blau, S., Marx, N., Breengill, L., Chambers, S.W. Prepubertal major depressive disorder, a pilot study. *Journal of the American Academy of Child Psychiatry.* 1978;17:695.
13. Freud, S. Mourning and melancholia (1915). In *The Complete Psychological Works, The Standard Edition, Vol. 14,* ed. and tr. by J. Strachey, New York: Norton, 1976.
14. Pfeffer, C.R., Zuckerman, S., Plutchik, R., Mizruchi, M.S. Suicidal behavior in normal school children: A comparison with child psychiatric inpatients. *Journal of the American Academy of Child Psychiatry.* 1984;23:416–423.

Chapter Five

1. Freud, A. *Normality and Pathology in Childhood.* New York: International Universities Press; 1965.
2. Wynne, L.C., Cromwell, R.L., Matysse, S., eds. *The Nature of Schizophrenia: New Approaches to Research and Treatment.* New York: John Wiley; 1978.
3. McKnew, D.H., Cytryn, L. Historical background in children with affective disorder. *American Journal of Psychiatry.* 1973;130:1278.
4. Cytryn, L., Cytryn, E., Rieger, R. Psychological implications of cryptorchism. In: Chess, S., Thomas, A., eds. *Annual Progress in Child Psychiatry and Child Development.* New York: Brunner/Mazel; 1968:396–419.
5. Cytryn, L. Factors in psychosocial adjustment of children with chronic illness and handicaps. *Clinical Proceedings,* Children's Hospital, Washington, DC. 1971; 28:85–90.
6. Bowlby, J. *Attachment and Loss, II: Separation.* New York: Basic Books; 1973.
7. Harlow, H.F., Soumi, S.J. Induced depression in monkeys. *Behavioral Biology.* 1974;12:273–296.
8. Hinde, R.A. *Animal Behavior: A Synthesis of Ethology and Comparative Psychology.* New York: McGraw-Hill; 1970.
9. Soumi, S.J., Harlow, H.F. Production and alleviation of depressive behaviors in monkeys. In: Muser, J., M.E.P. Seligman, eds. *Psychopathology: Experimental Models.* San Francisco: W.H. Freeman; 1977.
10. Soumi, S.J., Harlow, H.F. The facts and functions of fear. In: Zuckerman, M., Spielberger, C.D., eds. *Emotions and Anxiety.* Hillsdale, NJ: Erlbaum; 1976.
11. Higley, J.D., Soumi, S.J., Delizio, R.D. *Continuity of social separation behaviors from infancy to adolescence.* Paper presented at the 7th meeting of the American Society of Primatologists, Arcata, CA, 1984.
12. Soumi, S.J. Social development in rhesus monkeys: Consideration of individual differences. In: Oliverio, A., Zappella, M., eds. *The Behavior of Human Infants.* New York: Plenum Press; 1983.
13. Soumi, S.J. Bereavement-like responses to social loss in monkeys. Presented at the Annual Meeting of the American Psychiatric Association, May 20–25, 1995, Miami, Florida.
14. Cytryn, L., Lourie, R. Mental retardation In: Kaplan, H.I., Freedman, A.M., Sadock, B.J., eds. *Comprehensive Textbook of Psychiatry III, Vol. III.* Baltimore: Williams & Wilkins; 1980: 2506.
15. Reite, M. Maternal separation in monkey infants: A model of de-

pression. In: Hanin, I., Usdin, E., eds. *Animal Models in Psychiatry*. Oxford: Pergamon Press, 1977.

16. Seligman, M.E. Fall into helplessness. *Psychology Today*. 1973;7: 43.

17. Seligman, M.E.P., Peterson, C. A learned helplessness perspective on childhood depression: Theory and research. In: Rutter, M., Izard, C.E., Reard, P.B., eds. *Depression in Young People: Developmental and Clinical Perspectives*. New York: Guilford; 1986:223–250.

18. Seligman, M.E.P., Abramson, L.Y., Semmel, A., von Baeyer, C. Depressive attributional style. *Journal of Abnormal Psychology*. 1979; 88: 242–247.

19. Sharif, N.A., ed. *Molecular Imaging in Neuroscience*. New York: Oxford University Press; 1993.

20. Frazer, A., Molinoff, P.B., Winokur, A., eds. *Biological Bases of Brain Function and Disease*. New York: Raven Press; 1994.

21. Kupferman, I. Modulatory actions of neurotransmitters. *Annual Review of Neuroscience*. 1979;2:447–465.

22. Cooper, J.R., Bloom, F.E., Roth, R.H. *The Biochemical Basis of Neuropharmacology, 6th Edition*. New York: Oxford University Press; 1991.

23. Strange, P.G. The structure and mechanisms of neurotransmitter receptors. *Biochemistry Journal*. 1988;249:309.

24. Levitan, I.B., Kauzmamek, L.K. *The Neuron: Cell and Molecular Biology*. New York: Oxford University Press; 1991.

25. Puig-Antich, J. Psychobiological markers: Effects of age and puberty. In: Rutter, M., Izard, C.E., Read, P.B., eds. *Depression in Young People*. New York: Guilford; 1986:341–369.

26. Puig-Antich, J., Goetz, R., Hanlon, C., Tabrizi, M.A., Davies, M., Weitzman, E. Sleep architecture and REM sleep measures in prepubertal major depressives: Studies during recovery from a major depressive episode in a drug free state. *Archives of General Psychiatry*. 1983;40:187–192.

27. Sachar, E.J., Puig-Antich, J., Ryan, N., Asnis, G.M., Rabinovich, H., Davies, M., Halpern, F.S. Three tests of cortisol secretion in adult endogenous depressives. *Acta Psychiatricia Scandinavica*. 1985; 71:1–8.

28. Stokes, P.E., Stoll, P.M., Koslow, S.H., Maas, J.W., Davis, J.M., Swann, A.C., Robins, E. Pretreatment DST and hypothalamic-pituitary-adrenocortical function in depressed patients and comparison groups. *Archives or General Psychiatry*. 1984;41:257–270.

29. Asnis, G.M., Sachar, E.J., Halbreich, U., Nathan, R.S., Novacenko, H., Ostrow, L.C. Cortisol secretion in relation to age in major depression. *Psychosomatic Medicine*. 1981;43:235–242.

30. Robins, D.R., Alessi, N.E., Yanchyslyn, G.W., Colfer, M. Preliminary report on the dexamethasone suppression test in adolescents. *American Journal of Psychiatry*. 1982;139:942–943.

31. Amsterdam, J.D., Maislin, G. Comparison of growth hormone response after clonidine and insulin hypoglycemia in affective illness. *Biological Psychiatry*. 1990;28:308–314.

32. Amsterdam, J.D., Maislin, G. Hormonal responses during insulin induced hypoglycemia in manic-depressed, unipolar depressed and healthy control subjects. *Journal of Clinical Endocrinological Metabolism*, 1991, 73:541–548.

33. Ensen, J.B., Garfinkel, B.D. Growth hormone dysregulation in children with major depressive disorder. *Journal of the American Academy of Child and Adolescent Psychiatry*. 1990;29:295–301.

34. Ryan, N.D., Dahl, R.E., Birmaher, B., Williamson, D.E., Ivengar, S., Nelson, B., Puig-Antich, J., Perel, J.M. Stimulatory test of growth hormone secretion in prepubertal major depression: Depressed versus normal children. *Journal of the American Academy of Child and Adolescent Psychiatry*. 1994;35:824–833.

35. Cytryn, L., McKnew, D.H., Logue, M., Desai, R.B. Biochemical correlations of affective disorders in children. *Archives of General Psychiatry*. 1974;31:659–661.

36. McKnew, D.H., Cytryn, L. Urinary metabolites in chronically depressed children. *Journal of the American Academy of Child and Adolescent Psychiatry*. 1979;18:148–152.

37. Maas, J.W., Dekermenjian, H., Fawcett, J. Catecholamine metabolism, depression and stress. *Nature* (London). 1971;230:330–331.

38. McKnew, D.H., Cytryn, L., Rapoport, J., Buchsbaum, M., Gershon, E.S., Lamour, M., Hamovit, J. Lithium in children of lithium responding parents. *Psychiatry Research*. 1981;4:171–180.

39. Buchsbaum, M.S. The average evoked potential response technique in differentiation of bipolar, unipolar and schizophrenic disorders. In: Akiskal, H., ed. *Psychiatric Diagnosis: Exploration of Biological Criteria*. New York: Spectrum; 1978.

40. Gershon, E.S., Nurnberger, J., Nadi, N.S., Beretiui, W.H., Goldin, L.R. *The Origins of Depression: Current Concepts and Approaches*. New York: Springer Verlag; 1982.

41. Rosenthal, D. *Genetic Theory and Human Behavior*. New York: McGraw-Hill; 1970.

42. Wender, P.H., Kety, S.S., Rosenthal, D., et al. Psychiatric disorders in the biological and adoptive families of adopted individuals with affective disorders. *Archives of General Psychiatry*. 1986;43:923–929.

43. Blehar, M.C., Weissman, M.M., Gershon, E.S., Hirschfeld, R.M.A. Family and genetic studies of affective disorders. *Archives of General Psychiatry*. 1988;45:289–295.

Chapter Six

1. Mrazek, P., Haggerty, R.J., eds. Risk and protective factors for the onset of mental disorders. In: *Reducing Risks for Mental Disorders:*

Frontiers for Preventive Intervention Research, Institute of Medicine, Washington, DC: National Academy Press; 1994.

2. Gershon, E.S., Bunney, W.E., Jr., Leckman, J.F., van Eerdewech, M., DeBauche, B.A. The inheritance of affective disorders: A review of data and of hypotheses. *Behavioral Genetics.* 1976;6:227.

3. McKnew, D.H., Cytryn, L., Efron, A.M., Gershon, E.S., Bunney, W.E., Jr. Offspring of manic-depressive patients. *British Journal of Psychiatry.* 1979;134:148.

4. Cytryn, L., McKnew, D.H., Bartko, J.J., Lamour, M., Hamovit, J. Offspring of patients with affective disorders, II. *Journal of American Academy of Child Psychiatry.* 1982;21:389.

5. Beardslee, W.R., Wheelock, I. Children of parents with affective disorders: Empirical findings and clinical implications. In: Reynolds, W.R., Johnston, H.F., eds. *Handbook of Depression in Children and Adolescents.* New York: Plenum; in press.

6. Downey, G., Coyne, J.C. Children of depressed parents: An integrative review. *Psychological Bulletin.* 1990;180:50–76.

7. Rutter, M. Commentary: Some focus on process consideration regarding effects of parental depression on children. *Development Psychology.* 1990;26:60–67.

8. Wallerstein, J.S. The long-term effects of divorce on children: A review. *American Journal of Child and Adolescent Psychiatry.* 1991;30: 346–360.

9. Geller, B., Fox, L.W., Clark, K.A. Rate and predictors of prepubertal bipolarity during follow-up of six to twelve year old depressed children. *Journal of the American Academy of Child and Adolescent Psychiatry.* 1994;33:461–468.

10. Kovacs, M., Akiskal, H.S., Gatsonis, C., Parrone, P.L. Childhood onset dysthymic disorder: Clinical features and prospective naturalistic outcome. *Archives of General Psychiatry.* 1994;51:365–374.

11. Apter, A., Borengasser, M.A., Hamovit, J., Bartko, J.J., Cytryn, L., McKnew, D.H. A four-year follow-up of depressed children. *Journal of Preventive Psychiatry.* 1982;1:89.

12. Poznanski, E.O., Krahenbuhl, V., Zrull, J.P. Childhood depression: A longitudinal perspective. *Journal of the American Academy of Child Psychiatry.* 1976;15:491.

13. Anthony, E.J., Cohler, B.J., eds. *The Invulnerable Child.* New York: Guilford; 1987.

14. Shekim, W.P., Hardin, C., Kashani, K., Hodges, K.K., Cytryn, L., McKnew, D.H. *Depression in Hyperactive Boys.* Paper presented at the Annual Meeting of the American Academy of Child Psychiatry, Chicago, 1980.

15. McClellan, J.M., Rupert, M.P., Reichler, R.J., Sylvester, C.E. Attention deficit disorder in children at risk for anxiety and depression. *Journal of the American Academy of Child and Adolescent Psychiatry.* 1990;29:534–539.

16. Kashani, J., Manning, G., McKnew, D.H., Cytryn, L., Husain, A.,

Wooderson, P. Depression among incarcerated delinquents. *Psychiatry Research.* 1980;3:185.

17. Aber, J.L., Allen, J.P. The effects of maltreatment on young children's socioemotional development. *Developmental Psychology.* 1987;23:406–414.

18. Comstock, G.W., Helsin, K.J. Symptoms of depression in two communities. *Psychological Medicine.* 1976;6:551–563.

19. Craig, T.J., Van Natta, P.A. Influence of demographic characteristics on two measures of depressive symptoms: The relation of prevalence and persistence of symptoms with sex, age, education, and marital status. *Archives of General Psychiatry.* 1979;36:149–154.

20. Radloff, L.S., Rea, D.S. Susceptibility and precipitating factors in depression: Sex differences and similarities. *Journal of Abnormal Psychology.* 1979;88:174–181.

21. Steels, R.E. Relationship of race, sex, social class, and social mobility to depression in normal adults. *Journal of Social Psychology.* 1978; 104:37–47.

22. Weissman, M.M., Klerman, G.L. Sex differences and the epidemiology of depression. *Archives of General Psychiatry.* 1977;34:98–111.

23. Clayton, P. Bipolar affective disorder: Techniques and results of treatment. *American Journal of Psychotherapy.* 1978;32:81–92.

24. Regier, D.A., Boyd, J.H., Burke, J.D., Rae, D.S., Myers, J.K., Kramer, M., Robins, L.N., George, A.K., Karno, M., Locke, B.Z. One-month prevalence of mental disorders in the United States. Based on five Epidemiologic Catchment Area Sites. *Archives of General Psychiatry.* 1988;45:977–986.

25. Bruce, M.L., Takenchi, D.T., Leaf, P.J. Poverty and psychiatric status: Longitudinal evidence from the New Haven Epidemiologic Catchment Area Study. *Archives of General Psychiatry.* 1991;45:977–986.

26. Kaplan, G.A., Roberts, R.E., Camacho, T.C., Coyne, J.C. Psychosocial predictors of depression: Prospective evidence from the Human Population Laboratory Studies. *American Journal of Epidemiology.* 1987;125:206–220.

27. Hough, R.L., Landsverk, J.A., Karno, M., Burnam, M.A., Timbers, D.M., Escobar, J.I., Regier, D.A. Utilization of health and mental health services by Los Angeles Mexican Americans and non-Hispanic whites. *Archives of General Psychiatry.* 1987;44:702–709.

28. Cadman, D., Boyle, M.H., Offord, D.R., Szatmari, P., Rae-Grant, N., Crawford, J.W., Byles, J.A. Chronic illness and functional limitation in Ontario children. Findings of the Ontario Child Health Study. *Journal of the Canadian Medical Association.* 1986;135:761–767.

29. Cytryn, L., Lourie, R. Mental retardation. In: Kaplan, H.I., Freedman, A.M., Sadock, B.J., eds. *Comprehensive Textbook of Psychiatry, III, Vol. III.* Baltimore: Williams & Wilkins; 1980:2506.

30. Beardslee, W.R., Podorefsky, D. Resilient adolescents whose par-

ents have serious affective and other psychiatric disorders: Importance of self-understanding and relationships. *American Journal of Psychiatry.* 1988;145:63–69.

31. Pellegrini, D.S., Nachman, D., Kosisky, S., Caminso, K., Cytryn, L., McKnew, D.H. *Children at risk for depression: Psychiatric and psychosocial functioning.* Presented at the annual meeting of the American Psychological Association, Anaheim, CA 1983.
32. Brown, G.W., Harris, T.O. Depression. In: Brown, G.W., Harris, T.O., eds. *Life Events and Illness.* New York: Guilford; 1989.
33. Cytryn, L., McKnew, D.H. Treatment of childhood depression. In: Noshpitz, J., ed. *Basic Handbook of Child Psychiatry.* New York: Basic Books; 1987:439–442.

Chapter Seven

1. Winnicott, D.W. *Collected Papers.* New York: Basic Books; 1958:204–218.
2. Beck, A.T., Rush, A.J., Shaw, B.F., Emery, G. *Cognitive Therapy in Depression.* New York: Guilford; 1979.
3. Kovacs, M., Beck, A.T. An empirical-clinical approach toward a definition of childhood depression. In: J.G. Schultenbrandt, J.G., Raskin, A., eds. *Depression in Childhood.* New York: Raven Press; 1977.
4. Klerman, G.L., Weissman, M.M., Rounsaville, B.J., Chevron, E.S. *Interpersonal Psychotherapy of Depression.* New York: Basic Books; 1984.
5. Levy, D. Release therapy. *American Journal of Orthopsychiatry.* 1939;9:713.
6. Allen, F.H. *Psychotherapy with Children.* New York: Norton; 1942.
7. Alexander, F., French, T. *Psychoanalytic Therapy: Principles and Applications.* New York: Ronald Press; 1946.
8. Freud, A. Introduction to the technique of child analysis. *Nervous and Mental Disease Monograph.* 1929; 48.

Chapter Eight

1. Muller, J.C., Pryer, W.W., Gibbons, J.E., Orgain, E.S. Depression and anxiety occurring during rauwolfia therapy. *Journal of the American Medical Association.* 1955;159:836.
2. Lemieux, G., Davignon, A., Genest, J. Depressive states during rauwolfia therapy for arterial hypertension: A report of thirty cases. *Canadian Medical Association Journal.* 1956;74:522.
3. Harris, T.H. Depression induced by rauwolfia compounds. *American Journal of Psychiatry.* 1957;113:950.
4. Brodie, B.B. Some ideas on the mode of action of imipramine-type antidepressants. In: Marks, J., Pare C.M.B., eds. *The Scientific Basis of Drug Therapy in Psychiatry.* Oxford: Pergamon Press; 1965.

5. Schildkraut, J.J. The catecholamine hypothesis of affective disorders: A review of supporting evidence. *American Journal of Psychiatry*. 1965;122:509.

6. Schildkraut, J.J., Kety, S.S. Biogenic amines and emotion. *Science*. 1967;156:21.

7. Lapin, I.P., Oxenburg, G.F. Intensification of the central serotonergic processes as a possible determinant of the thymoleptic effect. *Lancet*. 1969;1:132.

8. Kuhn, R. Ueber kindliche depressionen und ihre behandlung. *Schweizerische Medicin*. Wochenschrift; 1963;93:86.

9. Kline, N.S. *From Sad to Glad*. New York: Ballantine Books; 1974.

10. Cade, J.F.J. Lithium salts in the treatment of psychotic excitement. *Medical Journal of Australia*. 1949;36:349–352.

11. Schou, M. Lithium in psychiatric therapy and prophylaxis. *Journal of Psychiatric Research*. 1968;6:67–95.

12. Preskorn, S.H. Advances in antidepressant pharmacotherapy. *Psychiatric Times*. June, 1995.

13. Preskorn, S.H. Antidepressant drug selection: Criteria and options. *Journal of Clinical Psychiatry*. 1994;55:6–22.

14. Prien, R.F., Kupfer, D.J. Continuation drug therapy for major depressive episodes: How long should it be maintained? *American Journal of Psychiatry*. 1986;143:18–32.

15. Kupfer, D.J., Frank, E., Perel, J.M., et al. Five-year outcome for maintenance therapies in recurrent depression. *Archives of General Psychiatry*. 1992;49:769–773.

16. Nelson, J.C., Mazure, C.M., Bowers, M.B., Jatlow, P.I. A preliminary, open study of the combination of fluoxetine and desimipramine for rapid treatment of major depression. *Archives of General Psychiatry*. 1991;48:303–307.

17. Schou, M. *Lithium Treatment of Manic-Depressive Illness: A Practical Guide, 5th Edition*. New York: S. Karger; 1993.

18. Kramer, P. *Listening to Prozac*. New York: Penguin; 1994.

19. *Clinical Psychiatry News*, July 1995.

20. Geller, B. Longitudinal studies of depressive disorders in children. *Journal of the American Academy of Child and Adolescent Psychiatry*. 1993;32:7.

21. Kovacs, M., Feinberg, T.L., Crouse-Novak, M.S., Palilaskas, S.L., Finkelstein, R. Depressive disorders in childhood, II. A longitudinal study of the risk for a subsequent major depression. *Archives of General Psychiatry*. 1984;41:643–649.

22. Ambrosini, P.J., Bianchi, M.D., Rabinovich, H., Elia, J. Antidepressant treatment in children and adolescents with affective disorders. *Journal of the American Academy of Child and Adolescent Psychiatry*. 1993;32:1–6.

23. Ryan, N.D. Heterocyclic antidepressants in children and adolescents. *Journal of Child and Adolescent Psychopharmacology*. 1990;1:21–32.

24. Ambrosini, P.J. Pharmacotherapy in child and adolescent major de-

pressive disorder. In: Meltzer, H.T., ed. *Psychopharmacology: The Third Generation of Progress.* New York: Raven Press; 1987:1247–1254.

25. Jensen, P.S., Ryan, N.D., Prien, R. Psychopharmacology of child and adolescent major depression: Present status and future directions. *Journal of Child Adolescent Psychopharmacology.* 1992;2:31–48.

26. Elliot, G.R. Dilemmas for clinicians and researchers using antidepressants to treat adolescents with depression. *Journal of Child Adolescent Psychopharmacology.* 1992;2:7–10.

27. Strober, M. Relevance of early age-of-onset in genetic studies of bipolar affective disorder. *Journal of the American Academy of Child and Adolescent Psychiatry.* 1992;4:606–610.

28. Popper, C.W. Are clinicians ahead of researchers in finding a treatment for adolescent depression? *Journal of Child and Adolescent Psychopharmacology.* 1992;2:1–4.

29. Riddle, M.A., Nelson, J.C., Kleinman, C.S., Rasmusson, A., Leckman, J.F., King, R.A., Cohen, D.J. Case study: Sudden death in children receiving norpramin. A review of three reported cases and commentary. *Journal of the American Academy of Child and Adolescent Psychiatry.* 1991;30:104–108.

30. Tingelstad, J.B. The cardiotoxicity of the tricyclics. *Journal of the American Academy of Child and Adolescent Psychiatry.* 1991;30:845–846.

31. Alessi, N., Naylor, M.W., Ghaziudinn, M., Zubieta, J.K. Update on lithium carbonate therapy in children and adolescents. *Journal of the American Academy of Child and Adolescent Psychiatry.* 1994;33:291–304.

32. McKnew, D.H., Cytryn, L., Rapoport, J., Buchsbaum, M., Gershon, E., Lamour, M., Hamovit, J. Lithium in children of lithium-responding parents. *Psychiatry Research.* 1981;4:171.

33. DiMascio, A., Weissman, M.M., Prusoff, B.A., Neu, C., Zwilling, M., Klerman, G.L. Differential symptom reduction by drugs and psychotherapy in acute depression. *Archives of General Psychiatry.* 1979;36:1450–1456.

34. Eckins, I., Shea, T., Watkins, J.T., Imber, S.D., Sotsky, S.M., Collins, J.F., Glass, D.R., Pilkonis, P.A., Leber, W.R., Docherty, J.R., Fiester, S.J., Parloff, M.B. National Institute of Mental Health treatment of depression collaborative research program: General effectiveness of treatment. *Archives of General Psychiatry.* 1989;46:971–982.

35. Goodwin, F.K., Jamison, K.R. *Manic Depressive Illness.* New York: Oxford University Press, 1990.

36. Jamison, K.R. Manic-depressive illness: The overlooked need for psychotherapy. In: Beitman, B.D., Klerman, G.L., eds. *Integrating Pharmacotherapy and Psychotherapy.* Washington, DC: American Psychiatric Press; 1991.

37. American Psychiatric Association: Practice guideline for major depressive disorder in adults. *American Journal of Psychiatry.* 1993; 150:1–26.

38. American Psychiatric Association: Practice guideline for the treatment of patients with bipolar disorder. *American Journal of Psychiatry, Supplement.* 1994;151:1–36.

Chapter Nine

1. Murphy, L. *The Widening World of Childhood.* New York: Basic Books; 1962.

Chapter Ten

1. Cytryn, L., Lourie, R. Mental retardation. In: Kaplan, H.I., Freedman, A.M., Sadock, B.J., eds. *Comprehensive Textbook of Psychiatry III,* Vol. III. Baltimore: Williams & Wilkins; 1982:

2. Lourie, R. Foreword to McKnew, D.H., Cytryn, L., Yahraes, H. *Why Isn't Johnny Crying?* New York: Norton; 1983.

3. Wiener, J. Preface to Shaffer, D., Phillips, I., Enzer, N.B., eds. *Prevention of Mental Disorders, Alcohol and Other Drug Use in Children and Adolescents.* U.S. Dept. of Health and Human Services: Washington, DC. 1989.

4. Mrazek, P.J., Haggerty, R.J., eds. *Reducing Risks for Mental Disorders: Frontiers for Preventive Intervention Research.* Washington, DC: National Academy Press: 1994.

5. Baldwin, J. Report card assessing national plan for research on child and adolescent mental disorders. *Psychiatric Times.* April, 1995.

6. Comer, J.P. The Yale-New Haven primary prevention project: A follow-up study. *Journal of the Academy of Child and Adolescent Psychiatry.* 1985;24:154–160.

7. Beardsley, W.R., Keller, M.B., Lavori, P.W., Staley, J., Sacks, N. The impact of parental affective disorder on depression in offspring: A longitudinal follow-up study in a non-referred sample. *Journal of the Academy of Child and Adolescent Psychiatry.* 1993;32:723–730.

8. Beardsley, W.R., Salt, P., Porterfield, K., Rothberg, P.C., Van de Velde, P.P., Swatling, S., Hoke, L., Moilanen, D.L., Wheelock, I. Comparisons of preventive interventions for families with parental affective disorder. *Journal of the American Academy of Child and Adolescent Psychiatry.* 1993;32:254–263.

9. Wallerstein, J.S. The long-term effects of divorce on children: A review. *American Journal of Child and Adolescent Psychiatry.* 1991;30:346–360.

10. Lewin, T. Now divorcing parents must learn how to cope with children's needs. *The New York Times.* April 24, 1995.

11. Grych, J.H., Fincham, F.D. Interventions for children of divorce: Toward greater integration of research and action. *Psychological Bulletin.* 1992;111:434–454.

12. *Psychiatric Times.* May, 1995, p. 14.
13. Sherer, S. *Psychiatric Times.* May, 1993.
14. Downey, G., Coyne, J.C. Children of depressed parents: An integrative review. *Psychological Bulletin.* 1990;108:50–76.

Chapter Eleven

1. Cytryn, L., McKnew, D.H., Zahn-Waxler, C., Radke-Yarrow, M., Gaensbauer, T.J., Harmon, R.J., Lamour, M. Affective disturbances in the offspring of affectively ill patients—a developmental view. *American Journal of Psychiatry.* 1984,141:219–222.
2. Puig-Antich, J. Psychobiological markers: Effect of age and puberty. In: Rutter, M., Izard, C.E., Read, P.B. eds. *Depression in Young People, Developmental and Clinical Perspectives.* New York: Guilford Press: 1986;341–382.
3. Cytryn, L. McKnew, D.H. Affective disorders in childhood. In: Kaplan, H.I., Friedman, A.M., Sadock, B.H., eds. *Comprehensive Textbook of Psychiatry III, Vol. III.* Baltimore: Williams & Wilkins; 1980.
4. Asnis, G.M., Sachar, E.J., Halbreich, U., Nathan, R.S., Novacenko, H., Ostrow, L.C. Cortisol secretion in relation to age in major depression. *Psychosomatic Medicine.* 1981;43:235–242.
5. Lohmayer, H.W., Poznanski, E.O., Bellur, S.N. EEG sleep in depressed adolescents. *American Journal of Psychiatry.* 1985;140:1150–1153.
6. Pozanski, E.D., Carroll, B.J., Banegas, M.C., Sook, S.C., Grossman, J.A. The dexamethasone suppression test in prepubertal depressed children. *American Journal of Psychiatry.* 1982;130:321–324.
7. Ryan, N.D., Dahl, R.E., Birmaher, B., Williamson, D.E., Iyengar, S., Nelson, B., Puig-Antich, J., Perel, J.M. Stimulatory tests of growth hormone secretion in prepubertal major depression: Depressed versus normal children. *American Journal of Child and Adolescent Psychiatry.* 1994;33:824–833.
8. *The Clinical Psychiatry News.* July, 1995.
9. Alessi, N., Naylor, M.W., Ghaziudinn, M., Zubieta, J.K. Update on lithium carbonate therapy in children and adolescents. *Journal of the American Academy of Child and Adolescent Psychiatry.* 1994;33:291–304.
10. Kashani, J.H., Silva, T.A., Anderson, J.C., Clarkson, S.F., McGee, R.O., Walton, L.A., Williams, S.M., Robins, A.J., Cytryn L., McKnew, D.H. The nature and prevalence of major and minor depression in a sample of nine-year old children. *Archives of General Psychiatry.* 1983;40:1217–1227.
11. Petersen, A.C., Compas, B.E., Brooks-Gunn, J. *Depression in Adolescence: Current Knowledge, Research Direction, and Implications for Programs and Policy.* New York: Carnegie; 1992.
12. Kovacs, M., Feinberg, T.L., Crouse-Novak, M.S., Palilaskas, S.L., Fin-

delstein, R. Depressive disorders in childhood, II. A longitudinal study of the risk for a subsequent major depression. *Archives of General Psychiatry.* 1984;41:643–649.

13. Asarnow, J.R., Carlson, G.A., Perdue, S., Bates, S., Keller, J. Childhood-onset of depressive disorders: A follow-up study of rates of rehospitalization and out-of-home placement among child psychiatric inpatients. *Journal of Affective Disorders.* 1988;15:245–253.

14. Weissman, M.M., Gammon, G.D., John, K., Merikangas, K.R., Warner, V., Prussoff, B.A., Sholomskas, D. Children of depressed parents: Increased psychopathology and early onset of major depression. *Archives of General Psychiatry.* 1987;44:847–853.

15. McCauley, E., Myers, K., Mitchell, J., Calderon, R., Schloredt, K., Treder, R. Depression in young people. *Journal of the American Academy of Child and Adolescent Psychiatry.* 1993;32:714–722.

16. Rohde, P., Lewinson, P.M., Seeley, J.R. Are adolescents changed by an episode of major depression? *Journal of the American Academy of Child and Adolescent Psychiatry.* 1995;39:1289–1298.

17. Jensen, P.S., Ryan, N.D., Prien, R. Psychopharmacology of child and adolescent major depression: Present status and future directions. *Journal of Child and Adolescent Psychopharmacology.* 1992;2:31–48.

18. Spitz, R.A. Anaclitic depression: An inquiry into the genesis of psychiatric conditions in early childhood, II. *Psychoanalytic Study of the Child.* 1946;2:312.

19. Engel, G.L., Reichsman, R. Spontaneous and experimentally induced depression in an infant with gastric fistula. *Journal of the American Psychoanalytic Association.* 1956;4:428.

20. Bowlby, J. *Attachment and Loss, II: Separation.* New York: Basic Books; 1973.

21. Post, R.M. Transduction of psychosocial stress into the neurobiology of recurrent affective disorder. *American Journal of Psychiatry.* 1992;149:999–1010.

22. Kraepelin, E. *Manic Depressive Insanity and Paranoia.* Translated by Barclay, R.M. Robertson, G.M., ed. Edinburgh, England: Livingstone; 1921.

23. Post, R.M., Rubinow, D.R., Ballenger, J.C. Conditioning sensitization and kindling: Implications for the course of affective illness. In: Post, R.M., Ballenger, J.C., eds. *Neurobiology of Mood Disorders.* Baltimore: Williams & Wilkins; 1984.

24. Post, R.M., Rubinow, D.R., Ballenger, J.C. Conditioning and sensitization in the longitudinal course of affective illness. *British Journal of Psychiatry.* 1986;149:191–201.

25. Ambelas, A. Life events and mania: A special relationship. *British Journal of Psychiatry.* 1987;150:235–240.

26. Ghaziudinn, M., Ghaziudinn, N., Stein, G.S. Life events and the recurrence of depression. *Canadian Journal of Psychiatry.* 1990;35:239–242.

27. Weiss, R.B., Post, R.M. Caveats in the use of the kindling model of affective disorders. Presented at the conference on low exposure to chemicals and neurobiologic sensitivity. Baltimore, Maryland; April, 1994.

28. Dragunow, M., Currie, R.W., Fauk, R.L.M., Robertson, H.A., Jansen, K. Immediate-early genes, kindling and long-term potentiation. *Neuroscience and Biobehavioral Reviews.* 1989:43:301–313.

29. Post, R.M. Models for the impact of affective illness on gene expression. *Clinical Neuroscience.* 1993;1:129–138.

30. Post, R.M., Weiss, S.R.B. Nonhomologous animal models of affective illness: Clinical relevance of sensitization and kindling. In: Koob, G., Ehlers, C., Kupfer, D.J., eds. *Animal Models of Depression.* Boston: Birkhauser Boston; 1989.

31. Lemonick, M.D. Glimpses of the mind. *Time.* July 17, 1995.

32. Kotulak, R. Children's brains may change in response to stress. *Washington Post.* August 31, 1993.

33. Axelson, D.A., Doraiswamy, P.M., McDonald, W.M., Boyko, O.B., Tupler, L.A., Patterson, L.J., Nemeroff, C.B., Ellinwood, E.H., Krishnan, K.R.R. Hypercortisolemia and hippocampal changes in depression. *Psychiatry Research.* 1993;47:163–173.

34. McEwen, B.S., Gould, E.A., Sakai, R.R. The vulnerability of the hippocampus to protective and destructive effects of glucocorticoids in relation to stress. *British Journal of Psychiatry.* 1992;160:18–24.

35. Post, R.M., Weiss, R.B. The neurobiology of treatment-resistant mood disorders. In: Bloom, F.E., Kupfer, D.J., eds. *Psychopharmacology: The Fourth Generation of Progress.* New York: Raven Press; 1993.

36. Post, R.M., Weiss, S.R.B. Sensitization, kindling and anticonvulsants in mania. *Journal of Clinical Psychiatry.* 1989;50:23–30.

37. Levinson, P.M., Mischel, W., Chaplin, W., Barton, R. Social competence and depression: The role of illusory self perceptions. *Journal of Abnormal Psychology.* 1980;89:203–212.

38. Levinson, P.M., Steinmeta, J.L., Larson, D.W., Franklin, J. Depression-related cognition: Antecedent or consequence. *Journal of Abnormal Psychology.* 1981;90:213–219.

39. Schrage, M. For biotech mappers, nothing beats slipping into a nice pair of genes. *The Washington Post.* September 16, 1994.

40. Asimow, I. *The Intelligent Man's Guide to Science.* New York: Basic Books; 1960:530–531.

41. Carey, J. The gene kings. *Business Week.* May 8, 1995.

42. Gershon, E.S., Nurnberger, J., Nadi, N.S., Berrettini, W.H., Goldin, L.R. *The Origins of Depression: Current Concepts and Approaches.* New York: Springer-Verlag; 1982.

43. Rieder, R., Gershon, E.S. Genetic strategies in biological psychiatry. *Archives of General Psychiatry.* 1978;35:866–873.

44. Cytryn, L., McKnew, D.H., Zahn-Waxler, C., Gershon, E.S. Developmental issues in risk research: The offspring of affectively ill par-

ents. In: Rutter, M., Izard, C.E. Read, P.B. *Depression in Young People: Clinical and Developmental Perspectives.* New York, London: Guilford Press; 1986.

45. Marshall, E. Manic depression: highs and lows on the research roller coaster. *Science,* 1994:264:1693–1695.

46. Berrettini, W.H., Ferraro, T.N., Goldin, L.R., Weeks, D.E., Detera-Wadleigh, S., Nurnberger, J.I., Gershon, E.S. Chromosome 18 DNA markers and manic-depressive illness: Evidence for a susceptibility gene. *Proceedings of the National Academy of Sciences.* 1994;9:5918–5921.

47. Bettelheim, B. *A Good Enough Parent,* New York: Vintage Books; 1987.

48. DeMyer, M.K., Hingtgen, J.N., Jackson, R.K. Autism: A decade of research. *Schizophrenia Bulletin.* 1981;3:388–451.

49. Seligman, E.P. *What You Can Change and What You Can't: The Complete Guide to Successful Self-Improvement.* New York: Alfred A. Knopf; 1994.

50. Moffet, J. Blame your genes? *Pennsylvania Gazette.* 1994;162:8–11.

51. Conrad, B., Weidmann, E., Trucco, G., Rudert, W.A., Behboo, R., Ricordi, C., Rodriguez-Rilo, H., Fingold, P., Trucco, M. Evidence for superantigen involvement in insulin dependent diabetes mellitus aetiology. *Nature.* 1994;371:351–355.

52. Mann, C.C. Behavioral genetics in transition. *Science.* 1994;264: 1686–1689.

53. Plomin, R., Owen, M.J., McGuiffin, P. The genetic basis of complex behavior. *Science.* 1994;264:1733–1739.

54. Reiss, D., Plomin, R., Hetherington, E.M. Genetics and psychiatry: An unheralded window on the environment. *American Journal of Psychiatry.* 1991;48:283–291.

55. Cloninger, C.R. Unraveling the causal pathway to major depression. *American Journal of Psychiatry.* 1993;150:1137–1138.

56. Klerman, G., Lavori, P., Rice, J., Reich, T., Endicott, J., Andersen, N. et al. Birth cohort trends in rates of major depressive disorder among relatives of patients with affective disorder. *Academy of General Psychiatry.* 1985;42:689–693.

57. Dinwiddie, S.S. Psychiatric genetics and forensic psychiatry: a review. *Bulletin of the American Academy of Psychiatry and the Law.* 1994;22:3,327–342.

58. Kendler, K.S., Kessler, R.C., Neale, M.C., Heath, A.C., Eaves, L.J. The prediction of major depression in women: Toward an integrated etiologic model. *American Journal of Psychiatry.* 1993;150: 1139–1148.

59. Aristotle, Parts of animals. In Ropes, L., ed. *Aristotle: On Man in the Universe.* Roslyn, New York: Walter J. Black, 1943, 61–83.

60. Asimov, The mind. In *The Intelligent Man's Guide to Sciences, Vol. 2.* New York: Basic Books, 1963; 703–745.

61. Broca, P. Anatomie compareé de circonvolutions cerebrales, le grand lobe limbique et la scissure limbique dans la serie des mammiferes. *Revue D'Anthropologie.* 1878; 1:385–498.

62. Robinson, R.G. Mapping brain activity associated with emotion. *American Journal of Psychiatry.* 1995; 152:327–329.

63. Papez, J.W. A proposed mechanism of emotions. *Archives of Neurology and Psychiatry.* 1937; 38:725–743.

64. MacLean, P.D. The limbic brain in relation to the psychoses. In Black, P., ed. *Physiological Correlates of Emotion.* New York: Academic Press, 1970.

65. Andrew, E.R. A historical review of NMR and its clinical application. *British Medical Bulletin.* 1984; 40:115–119.

66. Kuperman, S., Gaffney, G.R., Hamdan-Allan, G., Preston, D.F., Venkatesh, L. Neuroimaging in child and adolescent psychiatry. *Journal of the American Academy of Child and Adolescent Psychiatry.* 1990;29: 159–172.

67. Cooper, R., Papakostopoulos, D., Crow, H.J. *Rapid Changes in Cortical Oxygen Associated With Motor and Cognitive Function in Man.* Aviemore, Scotland: Churchill Livingstone, 1975.

68. Bandettini, P.E., Wong, E.C., Hinks, R.S., Tikofsky, R.S., Hyde, J.S. Time course EPI of human brain function during task, activation. *Magnetic Resonance in Medicine.* 1992; 25:390–397.

69. Ogawa, S., Tank, D.W., Menon, R., Ellerman, J.M., Kim, S.G., Merkle, H., Ugurbil, K. Intrinsic signal changes accompanying sensory stimulation: Functional brain mapping with magnetic resonance imaging. *Proceedings of the National Academy of Science.* 1992; 89: 5951–5955.

70. Goldszal, A.D.F., Schweitzer, M., Toner, J., Feroze, M. Functional MRI of muscle activity: The "pump," "flex," and DOMS. Paper delivered at the 81st Scientific Assembly and Annual Meeting of the Radiological Society of North America, Chicago, November, 1995.

71. Fox, P.T., Raichle, M.E., Mintun, M.A., Dence, C. Nonoxidative glucose consumption during focal neurologic activity. *Science.* 1988; 241: 462–464.

72. Schweitzer, M. Personal communication, 1995.

73. Tamminga, C.A., Conley, R.R., Wong, D.F. Human in vivo receptor imaging. *American Journal of Psychiatry.* 1994; 151:639.

74. Keshavan, M.S., Kapur, S., Pettegrew, J.W. Magnetic resonance spectroscopy in psychiatry: Potential pitfalls and promise. *American Journal of Psychiatry.* 1991; 148:976–985.

75. Volkov, N., Tancredi, L.R. Biological correlates of mental activity studied with PET. *American Journal of Psychiatry.* 1991; 148: 439–443

76. Peterson, B.S. Neuroimaging in child and adolescent neuropsychiatric disorders. *Journal of the American Academy of Child and Adolescent Psychiatry,* in press.

77. Botteron, B.S. Neuroimaging in child psychiatry. *Current Opinion in Psychiatry.* 1994; 7:324–329.
78. Arnold, L.E., Stoff, D.M., Cook, E., Jr., Cohen, D.J., Kruesi, M., Wright, C., Hattab, J., Graham, P., Zametkin, A., Castellanos, F.X., McMahon, W., Leckman, J.F. Ethical issues in biological psychiatric research with children and adolescents. *Journal of the American Academy of Child and Adolescent Psychiatry.* 1995; 34:929–939
79. George, M.S., Ketter, T.A., Parekh, P.I., Horwitz, B., Herscovitch, P., Post, R.B. Brain activity during transient sadness and happiness in healthy women. *American Journal of Psychiatry.* 1995; 152:341–351.

Epilogue

1. Kaplan, A. A look ahead: Mental health in the 21st century. *Psychiatric Times.* April, 1993.
2. Baxter, L.J.R., Schwartz, J.M., Bergman, K.S., Szuba, M.P., Guze, B.H., Mazziotta, J.C., Alazraki, A., Selin, C.E., Ferng, H.K., Munford, P. Caudate glucose metabolic rate changes with both drug and behavior therapy for obsessive compulsive disorder. *Archives of General Psychiatry.* 1992;49:681–689.

Index